Vanishing Rural America

Life then and now on a small farm

A Memoir by D. Matzen

The Rural Gallery
Clinton, Washington
dcm@theruralgallery.com

The Rural Gallery Publishing

Clinton, WA 98236

ISBN: 9798387822742

Dedicated to the one I love,
Bob, my husband, who stands
by me in spite of my foibles.

Vanishing
Rural
America

Old Barn near Oak Harbor—Painting by D. Matzen

Introduction

"I would rather be on my farm than be emperor of the world."
– **George Washington**

I lived on a farm from childhood through college, and I pursued that type of life as an adult. Over the years, I have been alarmed at the rate that vast areas of farmlands in Washington State, and elsewhere, have been overrun by population growth and affluence. McMansions abound both where I live now and where I grew up. Farming has become a hobby and does little to sustain the population.

This book is a collection of small vignettes from my rural life as a child and as an adult. These stories, hopefully, will present a clear idea of what I mean when I say "Vanishing Rural America." I have used this theme for many years in my paintings, trying to capture the glories of old handcrafted barns and outbuildings, the charm of draft horses plowing fields, the essence of what used to be, but what is being destroyed as we transform farmland into industrial parks and residential cracker boxes and McMansions.

This is a memoir with a focus on how the rural country-side is vanishing. Hopefully, I am painting images with words that will help you "see," in your mind's eye, what I see when I paint that beautiful round red barn that is falling into neglect, or when I watch a demonstration of how to plow a field with an eight horse team. These things used to be a normal part of farm life. Now they are an anomaly, not the norm, and many folks from the burbs come to view the buildings and watch the processes that are foreign to most people in modern America, seeing it as quaint entertainment, rather than as a required function for everyday life.

I am still seeking that part of the world that is rural. Too often, if there are any services locally, doctors, dentist, lawyers, CPA, groceries, etc, there will be folks encroaching on the surrounding farmland. If there is a town of some size nearby, you can be sure that you will have close neighbors in no time.

When I moved to Whidbey, I bought some acreage and, for almost twenty years, had the place to ourselves. Early on, I met my future husband, Bob, and we build our cabin together on the acreage I purchased. Now I have neighbors all around, mostly within three hundred feet of my home where I have lived for the past forty-seven years. I had twenty years of peace and now I have loud radios, cars and motorcycles, barking dogs that wander through my yard and bother my livestock. I live in the burbs which once was rural. I had a quiet place to grow vegetables and raise animals. No more.

For at least the last thirty years, Bob and I have been seeking a place of quiet where I can raise produce and livestock unhindered by the behavior of neighbors or county zoning regulations, a place where we won't be taxed out of living there, a place of peace. Although we had that for twenty years, I think that perhaps this utopia we seek is just that, an unrealistic dream that is no longer available.

Many of these stories are funny, though some are sad, but all are about living a somewhat rural life, though never far from a city center where the burbs have encroached.

Retired In Waterville—Painting by D. Matzen

CHAPTER 1

Seeking a Rural Life in Modern Times

"Beliefs are the road we take to reach our dreams. Believe you can do something—or believe you can't—and you'll be right every time." Jodi Picoult in "Sing You Home"

All my young life I dreamed of being a pioneer. I wanted to live in the wilderness and make my own self-sufficient way, be reclusive.. Well how practical is that? Firstly, there were hardly any frontiers left in the Lewis and Clark sense. Secondly, how do you feed and clothe yourself in a comfortable manner? Alaska was always a choice, or possibly New Guinea. Perhaps modern pioneering would be a state of mind, not a location.

When growing up in a rural community, I would go out in the woods and collect small downed alder trees and try to build a log cabin that could be my retreat in the woods. I was probably in third or fourth grade at the time. Never had much luck as the trees fell over when they were pretty rotten. By the time you got a few stacked up, the bottom ones were breaking. Putting mud on to chink the interstices totally collapsed the structure. Then you just had a square pile of mud and sticks. I did have determination and would work at this structure for hours before giving up. I might have done better to dig a hole in the hillside a crawl in, not unlike some of the early homesteaders.

I found this kind of life intriguing. I did consider more remote and sparsely populated areas as an adult. I have wandered over the wilderness areas of Washington state for forty years still looking for that place where I can be "almost self-sufficient" with the help of good old Social Security.

I have been withdrawn from mainstream society most of my life, though I get along pretty well with almost everyone. I tire of politics and am intolerant of petty cliques and think that it might be just as well to remove myself from these aggravations. I think about that pioneer in me that has been thwarted to some extent most of my life.

Being sent to teach for a year in China felt a lot like pioneering. It was probably close. Preparation was like that of preparing for a major expedition. Working there required new way of thinking. The culture was so foreign that it was an education in changing your way of living. And.......it was so much fun. Each day was a challenge and, though it was work, it was one of the most exciting times of my life. I never wanted to come home. I was a pioneer at last, living in a new frontier.....for me. But that is another story.

Now days, I focus not on new frontiers, but on self-sufficiency. My husband and I live in a cabin, the closest thing in modern times to my early life ideal. My mother-in-law used to ask, “When are you going to move into a real house?” Probably never. Many times we have considered a move, but we are still here forty years later. It is small, with the main living area of 850 square feet. I do have a 600 square foot painting studio which is a real luxury. It’s totally filled to the brim with art related “stuff,” half of which I should throw out.

Our garden produces a lot of our food with enough to dispense to others. Early on I hawked the veggies just like I did in 3rd grade, but now the surplus goes to the local food bank. This year the bean crop wasn’t as great as in the past, but we managed to give away one hundred and fifty extra pounds, after filling our freezer with enough for us for the year. It is good exercise to have a large garden, but my friends shake their heads and wonder why I work so hard to produce more than I need. It’s probably because some years the crops haven’t been that great and I need to grow too much to be sure I have enough.

We make our own yogurt, crème fraîche, and ricotta. We love to get fresh milk when possible, but don’t have a cow or goat, and mostly have to make do with milk from the local grocery. I make jams, jellies, conserves, pickles, relishes, tomato paste, roasted tomatoes, tomato sauce. We grow greens in our greenhouse in the off season, hydroponically, and in the garden in the good season. I raise chickens for fresh eggs and sell the surplus. We eat the old hens as stewers if we can’t sell them. We don’t purchase prepared foods. Well I do purchase rolled oats. I guess someone prepared them, but you get the point.

I am a competent baker and bake bread a couple of times a week. Our waistlines show that. When I discovered Leahy’s No Knead method of making French bread, I was in heaven. I had been trying for forty years to achieve a chewy crust with translucent crumb and holes. I do this every week now and it is perfect. We love it, sometimes with rosemary or roasted garlic or both. Sometimes it is shaped into ciabatta or focaccia with Greek olives pressed into it and olive oil and kosher salt sprinkled on the top. Yum. Baking also includes special goodies like croissants, flourless chocolate decadence cakes and riciarelli, an Italian cookie that is mostly almond paste. Being self sufficient doesn't mean subsisting on beans and rice, though we consume those as well.

Sausages are another thing we really enjoy making. After getting sausage at the grocery that was so salty we had to dilute it in soup to make it edible, we decided to grind our own. After living in China we enjoyed many dishes that took ground pork that was unseasoned in the western way. It was hard to get unseasoned sausage where we live, so we started making our own. We could also control the fat content this way. For breakfast sausage, we use lower fat ground pork and add a little olive oil to the mix to make it somewhat healthier. Chorizo is another we enjoy and we can make it with a good deal less fat than that which is sold in the store. We love rabbit and used to raise our own to eat. We like venison and occasionally are gifted some from friends as I haven't managed to convince myself to shoot the ones who come for apples on our farm. They do look tasty though.

In the cool season, I cook on a woodstove made by Wenkle in the 1930s. I love it and it keeps the house warm too. I call it the behemoth as it is five feet plus wide and over 5 feet tall. It is the place to age the cream for the crème fraîche and yogurt. It has a 5 gallon water jacket which heats water and gives off heat all night. Right now it is twenty-one degrees outside and we are toasty. It does require fuel and splitting wood is my autumn job. My husband cuts the wood and I split it. For years I did this chore with an ax and a splitting maul. About twelve years ago I invested in a splitter which runs off the hydraulics on our tractor and now I do it hydraulically. Yeah! I can split half a cord in the morning, but not before breakfast!

I used to do a lot of hiking and spend a lot of time in the wilderness trying to get my "pioneer fix" but now my yard is kind of a wilderness in its own way. I am trying to keep the woods from encroaching upon my gardens. Blackberries try to cover everything, along with nettles, buttercups, and a lot of other noxious natives. The deer had a field day with my hostas this year. They even ate the ones directly under my bedroom window. Rabbits weren't too bad this year and, so far, the raccoons haven't eaten my chickens. The coyotes are out howling in the woods, but we don't let the dog go out by himself and we no longer have a cat. We do have a peahen (the female form of peacock) that adopted us early one summer and has stayed. She liked the companionship of the chickens. She hated the snow however. The snow is a rarity here. She didn't seem to be too rough on the gardens, though she ate all the blossoms off the fuchsia bush as soon as they appeared.

Some years, water pipes freeze in the cold weather, power outages happen (twice so far during this snow), the rain barrel is frozen (no water available to flush the toilet during the power outage), the animals require that I go out with hot water several times a day to refresh their water supply which has frozen over. I could get water heaters for their waterers, but it happens so seldom it is hardly worth the investment, though during a power outage, they wouldn't work!

I suppose I could go out to show my pioneer spirit and build an igloo or snow fort and really be pioneering. I think I am a little old for that now. I do have a friend who is about my age who goes snow camping and she teaches people how to build snow caves to protect themselves if they are lost or a storm comes up while winter hiking, but she is a "better man than I,....." (Kipling)

I have read of folks who go to places and discover new species of plants and animals. I even thought of sailing around the world as a form of pioneering, but I get too seasick and I am afraid of sailing in storms. I am an armchair explorer via books, not television (we haven't had one for forty years). I can't say that I have taken a path that was disappointing as it has been rewarding and fulfilling, even if not financially; money isn't everything, but it helps. I may not be a pioneer in the strictest sense of the word, more an anachronism, but I certainly have had adventures in my life.

The First Farm-Deon in front of Mom's flowers—about 1955

CHAPTER 2

Who am I?

"The ultimate goal of farming is not the growing of crops, but the cultivation and perfection of human beings." – Masanobu Fukuoka

Who am I? I am an anachronism. I live in a small cabin. I chop and heat my cabin with wood. I cook on a wood cookstove. I grow my own food, I was twice a chef and prepare meals you would never think to eat at home. We eat well, too well.

We use and reuse what we have. I still wear clothes I purchased second hand forty years ago. We shop for most goods (except food) second hand. I only own two pieces of furniture that weren't purchased used. One is the mattress on my bed. We sleep outside in the summer and indoors in the winter. I have done this most of my life starting when I moved to a farm in fourth grade. After numerous couches (sofas) that were either too worn, or uncomfortable, we finally bought a new one. It is twenty-five years old now.

We may be classified as liberal, but in many ways we are very conservative. We save money and seldom indulge in extravagances unless it is extra-ordinary food, food I cannot prepare myself.

I make wine, grappa, yogurt, buttermilk, occasionally butter, salami, linguisa, copacola, bake croissants, slow cook dishes like casseolet on the stove. I often make our clothes of those not purchased second hand. I have made many of the rugs in our home. I have developed and made the lighting systems in our house. We have a new rock wall (3 tons worth) and fence completed recently by me.

Though some consider me anachronistic, I am savvy on modern technology. I can easily handle computers, cellphones, tablets etc. I can create many things in Adobe Photoshop and teach classes in the software.

Though I am going to soon be seventy-five years old, I consider myself active and creative. When tested in high school, I was deemed lacking in creativity, ranging poorly in the skills required to do problem solving creatively. Luckily, I did not receive that diagnosis from that five day concentrated test taken in high school until recently, so I was unaware I lacked creativity according to "them."I still find that determination preposterous.

The people who know and work with me would have trouble believing it. Many will come to me for problem solving of issues with unusual elements. Every day I work out problems of complex issues. I work hard to keep my mind active and creative, and I believe I am largely successful.

I am a painter by trade. I am a teacher by vocation, teaching people to develop their own creative skills through painting. Many are retired, feeling lost, with no direction in their lives. They come to me to teach them to paint. Most have gone on to be successful professional painters selling their work in the challenging art markets of today.

I am a reader (over 150 books a year) and a writer, writing being a new skill which I am acquiring a little at a time.

I am a twice stricken cancer survivor with a positive attitude to how much life may or may not have to offer me. If I have time, I will explore all I can.

I am a severely, but not profoundly yet, hearing challenged person who finds the challenges of hearing loss to be a major issue in my life. If I were to decide which was more challenging, hearing loss or cancer, I would tell you hearing loss.

Who am I? I am not sure, because evolving is a necessary part of a vital life, I change daily. I hope that I am always accepting of new challenges. I know I am becoming lazier as I approach three quarters of a century, but I am also rethinking my best direction to still be a vital and challenged person.

These days painting is my primary pursuit. I am particularly interested in color and am considered a color theorist. I paint realistically being a representational painter creating scenes from a specific genre—"Vanishing Rural America." This is not my only genre, but is my favorite and most prolific subject matter. My bread-and-butter topic is pet portraits and I have completed over two hundred dog portraits, a couple of dozen cats, a pig, several ducks and a Herford heifer.

I dabble in jewelry making as well, though this is more a hobby than a career. Mostly I work on these while I camp, in the evenings when it is dark or when it is raining and I am confined to my camp trailer.

I try to focus on these, though often I am tempted to take on other pursuits, things that peak my curiosity, but I need to focus and focus mostly on painting.

I learned years ago not to scatter my interest hither, thither, and yon allowing myself only to touch on different pursuits without focus. Now I am a painter and primarily a painter.

Today's Harvest

CHAPTER 3

Child Harvester

"To be a farmer is to be a student forever, for each day brings something new." -John Connell

My dad was from Nebraska and his family had a large kitchen garden in addition to raising turkeys and watermelons commercially. He missed farming when he relocated to California, thus we ALWAYS had a big garden the whole time I was growing up.

From an early age, I helped out in the garden whenever my parents were out there. We mostly raised a lot of vegetables. Living in Walnut Creek, California, we had good weather to produce a substantial garden which edged the south side of the house out to the street.

When I was about four years old, living in Walnut Creek, I knew my way around the garden pretty well. One day, it was about four in the afternoon and my mom was starting to prepare dinner. I don't remember what she was making, but she needed something from the vegetable garden.

I was sent on a mission to retrieve the particular item she needed for the dish she was making. Boy! I was going out to harvest something from the garden on my own. I felt very grown up and responsible. She even gave me a table knife to sever the treasure from its parent plant, maybe a patty pan squash, my favorite. I raced out of the house and headed across the driveway and down the walk to the garden. At the corner of the house was a downspout which drained the gutters whenever it happened to rain. It was frequently a little damp under the bottom edge of the downspout from the garden sprinkler hitting the gutter while watering the garden. It didn't rain much in Walnut Creek.

I raced around the corner of the house full tilt then came to a screeching halt. Something had caught my eye as I rounded the corner. There sitting in the cool dirt under the downspout was a coiled rattlesnake. It was a hot day and he had found a very pleasant place to stay cool.

We had occasionally had rattlers in the neighborhood and all the mothers would come out with brooms and beat the plantings around their houses to shoo them from the neighborhood, usually as a joint effort of several mothers.

I knew that snakes were bad, instinctively and because there was always a furor when one was in the neighborhood. That just reinforced my alarm. I suppose I didn't know that if it was coiled it could strike, I was too unschooled at that point to know, so I slowly, and sort of, calmly walked back past him and into the house.

"Where are the veggies you went out to get?" my mom asked.

"Mom, there's a snake out there by the corner of the house."

My mom dropped everything she was doing and peeked around the corner of the house. Sure enough it wasn't her child's overactive imagination. There was a rattlesnake dozing under the downspout.

Rather than alert the mothers of the neighborhood, and since the snake was in plain sight, she called the herpetologist who lived across the highway from our house. He came with a stick with a noose on the end. I GOT TO WATCH. He neatly snicked the loop over its head and carried it home. I guess he took it off to the university with him the next morning when he went to work.

Me, I have continued to grow veggies into my dotage, though now the snakes are friendlier in the maritime Northwest. Garter snakes are beneficial and eat slugs, my enemies. I still am startled by their presence, but I now can calm my pounding heart after first happening upon them. They are few and far between as the crows love to steal them when they are out in the open and the encroaching urban "wilderness" is wreaking havoc with them. Still they are beneficial and I try to encourage their presence in my gardens.

Eastern Washington Farm Truck—Retired--Painted by D. Matzen

CHAPTER 4

Farming memories

"The farmer has to be an optimist or he wouldn't still be a farmer." – Will Rogers

We first moved to the farm when I was in fourth grade. We didn't have any animals. They came later and along with them came the chores that are involved with keeping them happy.

One such chore came after the cows arrived. Cows make cow patties. These are dinner-plate sized, pudding-like piles that appear all over the pasture. The grass grows lushly around these piles, but the animals, cows and horses alike, will not touch it. It seems the smell of the waste does not make for palatable eating though the grass is beautiful and lush in a short circle around the patty. In many third world countries, when these piles dry out, they are used for fuel making an acrid odor while burning, but filling the need for fuel in an area where fuel is scarce. We were not THAT desperate. But, the available grass the animals would eat in the pasture was becoming reduced due to their abundance.

My dad had a company car which was a very fancy, low slung, peach-colored Oldsmobile sedan. One Saturday morning he drove into town and bought a set of bedsprings at the local junk store, the kind of bedsprings that are bare without fabric. We wondered why we needed this item and why he had bought them. Saturday morning came and he found a couple of very large rocks and a chain. The rocks were piled on the bedsprings and the chain attached. This, in turn, was attached to the Oldsmobile. My sis and I sat on the bedsprings as well. Around and around the fields we went, "dragging the pasture." This spread the manure to fertilize the whole field and do away with the areas the animals wouldn't eat. Thus our first farm equipment was an Oldsmobile tractor. Probably not the use his employer intended and somewhat reminiscent of the Beverly Hillbillies. I don't remember how much of the cow patties ended on my sister and me, but I think the dust was probably dense. We thought it was a hoot.

Once a year the youth group from our church would come to the farm for a summer picnic. We all loved to play volleyball, and we made sure that one team's side had plenty of cow patties to keep them at a disadvantage. There are several practical uses for these plentiful packages, giving the team advantage, fuel, and fertilizing the pastures.

When I was in college, we lived on a different farm. This farm had been the old Eddie Bauer homestead. The house was long gone, but some beautiful old plantings of lilac and locust trees, a modest lake and Bear Creek were still there. My folks built a new house along the creek which ran through the property. We could watch the salmon spawn every fall. My mom would take the pitchfork and collect the dead at the side of the stream, something that was terribly illegal, though she didn't know it at the time. She would bury them in the vegetable garden (an old Indian trick, she always said.

There were also trout in the creek. A fly fisherman would come around occasionally fishing in the stream walking though our property, in the creek, catching fish. Creeks and streams are open spaces and available to any who want to travel through them. My mom did not appreciate this invasion of our property and would decide that was the time to water the lawn, though the spray also would cover the creek as well, soaking the fisherman. After several episodes of this, one fisherman in particular approached my mom with a box. Inside were several beautifully cut glass goblets. It seems that he and his brother owned a famous glass cutting business in Seattle. They were gorgeous and purchased egress to our part of the creek any time he wanted from then on.

We also became friends with the fish and wildlife guys who monitored the creek. One fall they warned my mother that there would be activity near our house, about 100 yards upstream where the county road crossed the creek via a bridge. Sure enough that night there were search lights and a ruckus under the bridge. It seems that there were two fellows who came and gaffed the spawning salmon that were not too far gone and sold them to the public, also illegal. It was really some excitement for our neighborhood. My mother quit burying fish in the garden!

While living at the Eddie Bauer homestead, we had some peculiar activities at the neighboring farm as well. The man who owned this farm was a country gentleman. At one point he was offered an elephant, which he kept in his barn. He also had a camel, not your usual farm animals in the northwest. This gentleman farmer decided he needed a farm hand to tend his animals as he commuted to the city

(Seattle) weekdays. He went to the skid road area of Seattle to a bar and found a candidate. He asked the man if he gave him work, and a place to live, would he remain sober. "Sure!" was the reply. He worked diligently for several weeks, taking care of the animals, mowing the fields, rotating the irrigation pipes. It seemed he was very qualified to deal with the farm chores. Sometimes he would arrive at our house for a cup of tea and a chat as I think he was lonely in the countryside. Probably missing his fellow cronies from the Seattle bars.

One evening in winter the gentleman farmer came home and went to check on the daily activities of the farmhand. He was nowhere to be found. The hunt was on, searching the farm and hoping he hadn't had a tractor accident out in a field somewhere. The farmhand was found in one of the many taverns in the local town, about 8 miles from the farm. He just had to have a drink and the easiest means of conveyance available for him, not having a driver's license, had been the tractor. Driving a tractor doesn't require a driver's license.

Tractors can be very dangerous pieces of equipment and many lives are lost on farms each year due to overturned ones. Once when my dad was out working using the old tractor we had on the farm growing up, he got too close to the creek. The tractor started to tip. He turned into the tip and rode the tractor straight down the creek bank. Now he was in up to the hubs of the wheels in the creek. He had to drive to the nearest road to get back out. It was quite a ways down the creek to a road that had a low enough bank beside it to climb safely.

I have a tractor these days to help with projects around the property. About twelve years ago, I bought a splitter for firewood which runs off the hydraulics on the beast. One of the best investments of my life. I had been splitting wood with an axe and a maul, by hand for years and as my sixties approached, I decided I needed assistance with the chore. I spent $175.00 and it was worth every penny of it. I still use it every late summer and fall to bring in the wood for our winter's fuel.

When we first got the tractor, we didn't have a way to convey it from our other farm which is a good ten miles from our home. This entailed driving it back and forth. I will always wish that someone had taken a photo of me. Living in the greater Seattle area, there are coffee stands everywhere, even on rural Whidbey Island. Since I was getting cold and in need of a warm-up, I stopped at a drive-in coffee stand for my latte on the way home about four miles from my house. There I was on my tractor at the drive-in window. Quite a sight, but a good way to warm your hands while driving in the cold wind. You see, our tractor doesn't have a cab, so you are out in the weather when you drive.

Loons-Painting by D. Matzen

CHAPTER 5

Water

"When the well's dry, we know the worth of water." – *Benjamin Franklin*

Water and water rights are contentious topics. In modern times, we need to conserve, we need to ration, we need to change to help limit waste. In the community where I live we have limits, after which you pay through the nose for overages. So much for the 2500 acre feet per year allotment that was in effect when I arrived forty-five years ago. Imagine that much water, an acre being a little over 47,000 square feet!

Water has become precious. Hearing is also precious—at least to me. What do the two of these have in common? Good question.

When I was young I had acute hearing. I would hear sounds and could not figure out what they were. They were sounds of nature and sounds of the planet sighing and breathing. There were the sounds of water.

I didn't understand that I could hear water until I was probably in the seventh grade. That summer we were gardening in a place where we had no water to water the plants. We were dry land farming to some extent. Living in the Puget Sound basin doesn't mean that the land was parched, and for the most part spring brought volumes of rain.

As summer progressed the ground began to dry. We needed water for the vegetables. Intermittent rain could be expected, but the plants were wilting on hot days due to lack of water.

I thought I could hear water running or burbling in the ground. I know it is a preposterous idea. I suggested to my father that perhaps we could hand dig a well near the garden. He scoffed at the idea. I think he thought I was a little goofy. I insisted that I could hear water and we should dig in a certain spot to see if there was any there. He said, "You go right ahead."

I went to the barn and got a shovel. It was a warm day, and the soil wasn't too compacted. I started by digging a hole about twenty-four inches in diameter. It went fairly easily. I doggedly dug in pursuit of the water I heard in the ground. I needed to widen the opening as it became difficult to dig in such a confining space, thirty-six inches wide and eventually about forty inches.

Low and behold about four feet down the hole began to fill. It was filling quickly. I had found the water. It was probably that I had finally hit the water table level for that time of summer, but I HAD been able to hear the water.

Off to the barn to find a bucket. Back to the hole, I dipped and watered, dipped and watered and the water level seemed to subside and lower in the hole. I watered quite a bit, but when the level was about twelve inches from the bottom, I stopped. Within a half hour the level was back up to the rim and I finished watering the garden.

Several times over the course of weeks, I needed to clear the bottom of the hole as it was silting in. The water continued to come all summer to water the garden and was not necessary when the rains returned in the fall.

On other occasions I would be walking though a field and could hear water in the ground. Sometimes the farmer would be looking for a place to put a well, I would suggest that would be my choice and it would prove out.

How does this relate to hearing? Well, as water supplies diminish, so has my hearing. By the time I turned thirty-nine I had lost half my hearing and along with it, the ability to ferret out water for ourselves or others as I had done when my hearing had been acute. Now I hear only a small percentage of even the loudest voices without the assistance of hearing aids, I am classified as having severe hearing loss.

How does it feel to have a very unique skill taken from you? It was something that made me different, something special, and now I have joined millions of others who experience hearing loss. Though hearing aids help me survive in the modern world, the unique gift that I had now eludes me. It is sad in a way, that I have gone the way of water witchers and dowsers. Much more efficient systems are now available and technology helps us preserve the aquifer to protect the planet and its water supply.

I move on to a world of silence as the water below the land burbles.

PB&J—Painting by D. Matzen

CHAPTER 6

This is Not My Mom's Cooking

This is not for the faint of heart or those of tender ears….I mean, years.

I must have been in college when this happened. My sister was in junior high. We lived on the Eddie Bauer homestead, the home where Eddie Bauer, the outdoor adventurer lived, growing up, probably in the early 1900s. This was a few miles north of Redmond, Washington. I live many miles from that place now, on an island in Puget Sound.

Doc Nichols was a vet who lived at the other end of our road, about two miles from our house. He doctored our cows, horses and an occasional dog, though he was not a small veterinary practice, only large animals. He had been part of our lives for many years. In the beginning of our farming days, he had been the only vet in the area. Later there was another who handled a small animal practice, including dogs.

We raised Hereford cattle when I was growing up and Herford cattle sent me to college. I helped with difficult births, raised weaned youngsters and bottle fed beef growing up. Usually the steers had been “docked” at birth with the use of a judicious, very tight rubber band. Docked meant a form of castration. The calf was just born and the tight ligature was installed. Within a few weeks, the shriveled material fell off. This meant little or no pain to the animal.

Once in a while, my dad would decide to wait with this procedure to see if an animal developed as good bulls were hard to come by and were pricey to purchase, even ridiculous prices if they were particularly endowed.

One such juvenile bull didn’t seem to match up to the mark, thus the veterinarian; Doc Nichols’ services would be required to perform the castration. This entailed a more difficult procedure of removing the testicles though slits in the scrotum, not a painless procedure.

Part of Doc Nichol’s payment for the procedure was he kept the removed parts. He was partial to having these for dinner, but with the newer bands applied at birth, he didn’t often have the opportunity to perform the procedure or benefit from the results.

My dad called the vet to arrange for this less than perfect bull to become a steer so later he would be suitable for eating (unneutered bulls make for untasty eating). But…my dad made one stipulation. When the procedure was finished we would keep the by product.

My mom was irate. What was he going to do with these? He wasn’t cooking them in her house! This is barbaric. Who ever heard of eating animal parts while the animal was still walking around? How disgusting, how uncivilized. Not in her house. You need to remember that my mom was a Santa Barbara, California girl, though no longer a girl.

Well, the deed was done. We invited the vet to stay and partake as he had a particular affinity for this gourmet delight. I think that he passed as he knew there would be others (my young sister and myself) partaking of this banquet.

A barbeque was set up in a nearby field. Accompaniments were prepared. The meal would be a gourmet's delight. Two large ovoid-shaped pieces were placed on the grill and toasted to a crispy perfection. When removed they were sliced onto three plates, one for me, one for my sister and one for my dad. Things like mustard and horseradish were sides. I seem to remember coleslaw and other dishes too. We ate sitting in the grass around the "campfire." Thus were we introduced to Rocky Mountain oysters. They were delicious and crispy. In New Zealand and Australia these are called "fries" such as "lamb fries," etc. So if you are expecting potatoes in these countries, clarify the product that you wish such as "potato French Fries!"

I guess that this was to be part of our educations of growing up on the farm. I had been through castrating pigs, though we did not eat the by product. I had eaten the testicles of roosters from the farm and liked them, and now I had been introduced to beef testicles.

Needless to say, we didn't go into the house and talk about this gourmet repast as my mother was barely speaking about it or to us. She was so disgusted by the whole procedure that she was speechless, a rare thing for her. Dad was in the doghouse for hours and his young daughters had been indoctrinated into a school of experience she thought no young lady should experience in her lifetime.

Oh well, I really enjoyed both the actions of my conservative mother and the wonderful gourmet experience provided by my father. I still think on it this day five plus decades later.

The Old Smokehouse

CHAPTER 7

The Smokehouse On Whidbey

At one time (in the mid 1970s) I had quite a few 4 x 6" tongue and groove planks left from building my house. The longest of these were three feet. I had a stack of them. Growing up my dad had smoked many a meal on both outdoor grills and on the indoor grills built into our homes.

Well, being a frugal person not willing to waste any part of construction materials, I decided to build a smokehouse with the leftover planks.

When I built the smokehouse, I had the idea of stacking the tongue and groove to create a small building three by three feet with a door on the fourth side. My neighbors probably thought it was an outhouse as it looks very similar.

I dug a trench about fifteen feet long from the fire pit to the center of the six foot tall chamber. This was quite a feat as the area where I chose to do this we had used to dump refuse from the clearing of an area for an orchard, branches and tree stumps, blackberry canes and the like. The more I dug, the more tree stumps and miscellaneous materials I ran into in the course of digging the trench.

The idea was to have a firebox about fifteen feet from the smokehouse with concrete conduit leading to the inside of the new structure. This way the smoke from the firebox would be conducted up the slope from the firebox into the smokehouse and be cooled as it coursed upward.

I wanted cool/cold smoke. I didn't want to cook the items which were hanging in the smokehouse, only smoke them.

The main issue was to keep the meats cool so as to not allow them to decompose over the course of several days as the smoke rose from the firepit fifteen feet away.

I gathered alder saplings from hither, thither, and yon. I made a large stack that would last for many days, these having been cut to about twelve inches with the pruning shears to fit into the firepit which was dug into the ground.

It took a little tweaking to get the smoke to draw up the conduit rather than just going up from the firebox, but I finally found a way to heat the conduit so it would draw the smoke, filling it with paper and lighting until it would draw out the smokehouse itself.

One of my first projects was to smoke turkeys for an Island Arts Council fundraiser called Hogmanay, a winter festival celebrated, generally in December, in Scotland. Normally the featured dish would be haggis, a pig's stomach filled with an oatmeal/sausage-like material. Since this would probably not be popular with the folks of Whidbey Island, where I live, we decided on such dishes as galantine of sausage as enough pheasants were not available, meat pasties, and roasted smoked turkeys, along with other appropriate dishes, few of which celebrated vegetables as they were not popular at the Hogmanay Festival or in Scotland in general.

So here I had a brand new smokehouse. A very large stack of green alder saplings cut from a nearby clearcut, and time to smoke the turkeys over the next five days. Winter is the best time to do this as the outdoor temperatures are conducive to keeping the meats cool enough not to spoil.

You must be advised that even after five days of smoking, the meat was still raw and uncooked. This required sending the sixteen turkeys I smoked to different houses the day of the event to be cooked to the proper internal temperature.

I am absolutely amazed that we pulled it off. All but one of the turkeys were absolutely elegant and perfectly prepared. Fifteen were heavily smoked and unctuous and one was cooked in an early version of the microwave. This one looked as though it had been electrocuted. Tough and totally useless as food fare. There was a turkey for each table.

This event was held in a very old wooden building that was probably a fire hazard to begin with. We set each table for sixteen with white butcher paper, layered in evergreen boughs down the center of each, and placed dozens of red candles there as well. Fruits such as apples, oranges, and figs, were laid out and the platters of pork pies, pasties, galantine, and the roasted smoked turkey were placed in the center of each. There were flagons of wine and large trenchers of bread for plates. It was all very medieval in atmosphere. We had lute players with Elizabethan music and jugglers entertaining. People were encouraged to come in period costume.

I am still surprised that we didn't burn the place down.

The grand finale was dessert. We had sixteen servers, one for each table. I had steamed sixteen figgy puddings. These were placed on platters. Each server had a platter with a pudding on it. Whiskey was poured over each by one of the kitchen help and then the next kitchen person in the production line set it on fire and all sixteen servers set out to serve the guests.

Well, one tipped the platter and the kitchen floor was alight. Flames licked the floor. Luckily the flames from alcohol are easily extinguished and not very hot in nature. It was quickly put out. Onwards and upwards!

I must admit that the procession was quite spectacular as they paraded around the outer aisles of the hall before setting the flaming puddings on the tables. Everyone oohed and awed.

The whole project netted the Island Arts Council $600, which was a lot for the mid-70s. I had to take a month off to rest up and it was spoken of for several years. Now this event is long forgotten, but it gave a good boost to what today is the

Island Arts Council as well as the Whidbey Island Center for the Arts, which was originally sponsored by the council.

The smokehouse? For many years it was used to smoke bacon, ham, sausages and more. Now we have a more convenient and modern piece of equipment that does not require my running out every half hour for five days to toss on more alder saplings! I am getting too old for that.

Our original smokehouse is in dire need of repair. The shingle roof has decayed and is falling in, but the tongue and groove boards are still intact.

Samish Island Snow

CHAPTER 8

A Snowy Day

"Snowflakes are one of nature's most fragile things, but just look what they can do when they stick together." — Vesta M. Kelly

As I write this it is snowing. I am mesmerized; the large flakes float down, hypnotic. It has been a couple of years since we had snow and it is coming down onto very frozen ground. We had cold weather for a couple of weeks. This day, it warmed to thirty-three, the barometer dropped and the conditions were just right for snow. It is falling steadily, but not sticking anywhere, so it seems ethereal like it is only in the air, not on the ground or other objects outdoors. Very strange.

Western Washingtonians do not do well in snow. It is an unusual event. Usually the snow is very wet; though this day it is very light and dry, fluffy, drifting slowly from the sky. The light is almost opalescent. Most of us stay home if it snows. This is a good choice as most of the people here do not know how to drive in snow. I can drive in it having been a skier who spent time in the Cascade Mountains skiing, but the other folks who do decide to go out and drive may hit me while I am out. Luckily, we are always prepared for being stuck at home, be it from wind, floods, snow or the like. The cellar is full and the cupboards have enough to last several weeks. Water is a little short in ready supply as the rain barrels are frozen at the moment, but they can be thawed. Snow can be melted if enough builds up though a tedious process producing only small results.

A day like this always reminds me when we were young, my sister and I always wanted a sled. A sled is kind of a waste here in the Northwest as there is seldom snow enough to use it. We used to beg and beg my mother to let us have one, but the rule she made was we had to have six inches of snow before we could have a sled. When we awoke one snowy day, we had finally met the criteria and we tried to talk my mom into letting us have a sled especially since they had closed school and we were home to frolic in it.

She said sure we could have a sled, but she was not going to brave the elements or the treacherous driving to go into town to purchase it. We would have to walk to town four miles away. I suspect she was glad to be rid of us for most of the day. My sister and I didn't hesitate a second, we were ready in an instant, bundled to our ears. She gave us the money, though I don't know how she knew how much or even if the store was open, but we bundled up to walk the distance. We were excited, bounding along, kicking at the snow and really enjoying ourselves. We seldom saw anyone and we passed some good, steep hills that we planned to take advantage of on the return trip.

In town at the hardware store, there was not much choice as they had little call for sleds, even in winter. Not too many people even went out in the snow. I think Mom must have called ahead to be sure the store was even open and to ask the price. We plunked our money down and headed out with the sled. Going out of town was UP a very high hill, a really long haul which tempted us to give it a try. We passed knowing there were more inviting hills further along on the way home. It snowed off and on the whole trip, but we were warm and learning how to steer and use the new sled. We sledded and sledded and sledded the whole way home. Some of the better roads with steep hills we took four and five times. Our energy was beginning to flag.

When we got home, we had a couple of small hills by the house upon which we took a few passes, but after walking eight miles, we were bushed, to say the least. We slept well that night and the snow was gone when we awoke the next morning and had to go back to school. I think the sled rusted away in the barn as there was seldom the opportunity to use it again in the years that followed. I don't know why we never went to the mountains in the winter to sled, but we didn't. Kind of a sad story when you think about it. But still a fond memory on a day when the snow is coming down, even if it doesn't stick on the ground.

CHAPTER 9

The Behemoth

"Chop your own wood and it will warm you twice"—Henry Ford

It's true. If you own a wood stove and you chop your own wood, it will heat you twice. I generally try to chop my wood in late spring while the weather is still cool and the wood will have a chance to dry before fall, though sometimes, I must confess, I don't get to it until fall. It really does warm you, chopping wood. There is something wonderful about being outdoors on a cold crisp day and splitting wood. I love the deep turpentine-like smell of fir and hemlock as the pieces fall away. We also split alder occasionally which has its own astringent smell. It is good for smoking foods and imparts a wonderful taste. Fir and hemlock are not good for smoking unless you like a piney residue taste in your foods.

I used to split wood, for most of my life, with an ax. It was easiest if the trees were still green, and not dry, as the wood pops into two pieces more easily. I did this for years. Occasionally the ax would get stuck in a piece which wouldn't pop and that was when the real work began, trying to get it to pop by picking the whole thing up and bashing it down again to try to force the ax through, or just trying to loosen the ax from its confinement deep within the piece of wood.

Finally, as this was becoming more and more difficult, (for an old lady like me) I bit the bullet and bought a splitter to work off the tractor. It uses the hydraulics on the tractor to power a hydraulic cylinder that pushes a wedge through the wood just like the variety that is powered by a gas motor. Now all I have to do is be careful of my fingers and watch out if it pops violently, which it does sometimes. You can get nice bruises on your thighs if you are in the way. During the course of a morning I can split a half cord of wood if I am not stacking it as well. Boy was that a great $175 investment.

Now to the Behemoth. This is what I call my wood cook stove. About twenty or twenty-five years ago when my husband was in Montana visiting his family, he called and said he had located a stove in a barn in the eastern part of the state. It was in great shape. But.....did I mind that it was pink enamel? I was just happy for such a find. I said, definitely buy it. He brought it home and it is dove grey, a perfect color. My husband is red/green colorblind and he didn't really know what color it was and took a guess. I thought when he said pink it was probably the swimming pool green color that was popular in many stoves from the '30s.

It is a 1935+/- (?) Wehrle Colonial Range #82-20X. It had been sitting in a barn for a number of years when my husband purchased it and brought it back to Washington State where we live. It has heated our cabin ever since. When he purchased it, it had been converted to an oil pot burner, since there are not a lot of trees to burn in eastern Montana. Pot burners were a type of heating from Victorian times up until recent times. The local theater here on the island had a pot burner just in front of the screen that glowed on winter nights to keep the theatre warm. The cabin I bought when I moved here had an "appliance" which was enameled dark brown and sat in the living room. Classmates in high school had pot burners in their living rooms.

This device had a fire proof pot inside into which No. 2 stove oil (diesel) dripped at a rate set by a valve on the side of the device, by turning on the valve and letting a little oil drip into the pot. Open the door and drop a match or a piece of burning paper into the pot and the oil would ignite and heat the house as long as the valve was turned on. The amount of heat was determined by the speed at which the oil dripped. Outside there were barrels of diesel up on stands, higher than the pot in the house which were filled with oil that fed by gravity to the pot.

They worked well until oil prices skyrocketed and we could hardly afford to use them. In Montana, some enterprising farmer had converted this stove to this method of cooking and heating because he did not have access to trees and wood, and the stove was not useful for coal burning as it would become clogged with soot. When oil prices got too high, it had been relegated to the barn. Lucky us.

We, however, have enough windfall each year to heat several homes and this stove, after reconverting it back to wood, has heated ours easily. It includes a warming oven and water tank. There is also an accommodation for a water jacket, which we have not installed. We place a large box fan next to the stove to circulate the heat throughout the house. It is the only heat source we use and we are toasty. It bakes a great turkey or pot roast. I only use the oven for slow, low temperature cooking as the house gets too hot if I run the oven at anything higher than 275 degrees.

On the stove are three, three-gallon kettles. These are full of water which stays hot all night after the fire has gone out. They are still warm in the morning and the house is still toasty. When the power is down and our water pump doesn't run, these kettles are a source of hot water for washing up.

In winter the stove simmers a lot of soup. It is the perfect stove for this. I also make crème fraiche and yogurt in the warming oven. The mid-temperature (center of the cook top) burners are used to make ricotta cheese and it works better on this stove than on our gas range. We keep the tea pots warm on the top and coffee cups are stored and warm in the warming oven ready to use.

One of the burners on the top of the stove is a special pot lid with an insert that you can raise and lower so creamy soups and porridge won't stick or scorch on the bottom of the pan, which is real handy. It says on it "Raise register and cereals will never burn." I use this burner device to heat the milk for the ricotta. Never scorches on the bottom.

Not only is the Behemoth wonderful, but it does allow our chopped wood to warm us the second time.

The Ferry at Dawn—Painting by D. Matzen

CHAPTER 10

Working in Rural America

Mark Twain wrote, "Eat a live frog first thing in the morning and nothing worse will happen to you the rest of the day."

I moved to Whidbey Island when I was 27 years old. I was seeking rural America and I had found my niche on Whidbey. I still worked on “the mainland.” This required a commute daily by ferry. Back then there were a few of us who drove or walked-on the ferry to go to work. Little work was available on the south end of the island and unless you had a trust fund to keep you going here, a daily trip to the mainland was a necessity.

Bus service was non-existent on the mainland to take us from the dock to work, so various modes of transportation had to be arranged. I walked from my cottage one and a half miles down the beach to the ferry in the morning. Rode the ferry for 20 minutes, and picked up my car at a local free parking area on the mainland, doing the reverse on the way home. Hardly anyone lived in the cottages along my walk to and fro, and in the winter it was pitch black with lights only in one or two of the 50 or so houses on that stretch. Luckily the road was pretty level and very straight and my homing device just went to auto and off I went down to my house, seldom with the aid of a flashlight.

One winter was particularly wet and there had been many mudslides along the island's beaches. The road I walked had a continuous row of houses on the water side and a cliff covered in vegetation (mostly the briar patch of tangled invasive blackberries mentioned elsewhere) on the inland side. Usually, there was enough ambient light that I didn't use a flashlight to make the journey. One morning on my way to the ferry, I suddenly heard a horrific sound, but with no idea what it was. I continued walking, but couldn't imagine, possibly an earthquake. Ones I had experienced in the past had created a lot of noise. This sounded the same. Suddenly, behind me, thankfully, the whole cliff came whooshing down across the road, smashing the garage across the street. Later learned that it smashed the Mercedes SL garaged inside as well.

When walking home that evening, I viewed the damage and had to find an alternate route, so scuttled between two houses and finished the walk home on the beach in a pair of good heels that were ruined by the time I got home. Next time plan ahead. And, it did happen several more times. The problem is to know which way to run. Is it ahead or behind? Will I run away from it or into it? I guess just continue walking and hope it isn't your time.

Early one morning in winter when the sky was very clear, I spied five "falling stars" from the winter meteor shower. It actually happened two mornings in a row and I thought maybe I had imagined (being still half asleep) the whole thing, it was so spectacular. Maybe the show was just for me. Did anyone else spot that display at six in the morning? Probably not, as they were probably sleeping or commuting in their cars.

One pastime on the ferry is reading, but several people played cribbage on the boat. When we arrived at our destination, you just tucked the cards and board under the seat with the life preservers and resumed the game on the way home. Some of the games became very competitive and boisterous. Card players stationed themselves in one region and readers sat some distance away for quiet.

Another winter morning during a particularly wet winter (we have a lot of those), I stepped from my porch onto the path to head down the road to the ferry and sank into water almost knee deep. As my eyes had not yet adjusted to the dark upon leaving the house, I had not seen that the neighborhood was flooded. Back into the house for fresh pantyhose and shoes. Put my wet shoes by the furnace vent and started once again for the ferry, this time sans shoes and pantyhose, barefooted with skirt hiked up. I waded through the icy cold water for about a half block until I achieved the paved road which was set higher than the flood and continued on barefooted. It seems some building remodeler up stream had thrown the waste lumber from his home improvement project into the canyon up higher from my cottage. The materials had drifted downstream and jammed a culvert which had allowed the water to fill the neighborhood during the night. Luckily it did not get up to floor levels in my house and do any damage. Too bad it wasn't his house sitting in the water. When I got on the ferry, I washed my feet in the bathroom sink with gloriously warm water and tugged the pantyhose over my damp legs to be presentable at work. The flooding problem was alleviated by the time I returned from work.

On yet another very wet occasion, my car on the mainland, with which I was commuting at the time, was sitting knee deep in water when I arrived at the free parking lot. Again I had to peel off shoes and pantyhose and climb into through the rear compartment of my station wagon as it was too deep at the driver's door to wade. Again in winter when the water is about 40 degrees. A friend told me a lady told him, "Hey boy, if you go get my car for me I'll give you $5." Needless to say she was left standing at the edge of the flood. These are the type of folks moving here.

When I moved from that first house on Whidbey, I had more of a problem with the commute and working on the mainland as I could no longer walk to the ferry. At one point, I drove my car to a meeting point and parked, got into a carpool and rode the ferry, got into another car for another carpool on the ferry and rode to work. Four different modes of conveyance just to get to work.

When I first started the commute by ferry, the cost of a commuter card was equal to 16 cents per trip. The ticket taker punched your card as you got on the boat. At the early morning time I commuted there were three of us walking on and about six cars. It was easy and carefree. On one occasion, I was out of tickets and trying to catch the last boat, the window to purchase tickets had closed, but the deckhand just said, "Have the seller punch one for tonight when you purchase your new ticket tomorrow." Things were casual then. Now they won't even take a check! I also remember (in my younger days) almost missing the last ferry as it was leaving and the deck hand coming to the back and saying "jump!" which I did. It was only about three and a half feet, but the ferry HAD left the dock.

Sometimes the ferry couldn't run because of "technical difficulties." One time it couldn't dock because on the previous run a brand new Mercedes sedan with four passengers had had a little accident. When the ferry was unloading it had accidentally backed away from the dock somewhat. The four elderly folks, on their way to the airport, hadn't seen that an ever widening gap had appeared between the boat and the dock. Off went the front wheels into the abyss. The deckhands yanked open the doors and unceremoniously yanked out the four passengers just as the car tipped into the sea. What a way to start a vacation. Needless to say with a Mercedes parked on the bottom in front of the dock, the ferry couldn't get back in to finish unloading. No boat that afternoon.

There were also ferry worker strikes, one of which lasted a week. Since I didn't have vacation and I didn't think I could call in sick, I begged a friend to sleep on her couch for the duration. This entailed "driving around." This term means driving the entire length of the U. S.'s second longest island, crossing a bridge onto another island, crossing another bridge to the mainland, and then driving back down the mainland. The trip is a drive of about 110 miles to return to the place where you should have gotten OFF the ferry. My hostess wanted to party all week, so I was totally exhausted by the time I finally returned home.

There were storms as well. One ferry, during my first years of commuting, had an open deck with a little tower in which the first floor above the deck had two rows of seats fore and aft and the pilot house on the floor above (the Kulshan, now in NY harbor). One particularly bad storm, the boat rocked to such an angle that you looked directly into the water from your seat above the cars. One morning in such a storm there was a terrible crash. We tried to stand to look out. There was a large lumber truck parked on the deck in one lane with a row of cars adjacent to him. The straps on the load of lumber had strained seriously to the side and released the load on the cars. This gives a whole new meaning to the idea of having an accident on the commute to work.

During my later years of commuting, the island had become the "burbs" and commuting had become the norm with full loads of cars and hundreds of walk-ons. When we only had smaller ferries, there were so many walk on passengers that if you were not at the head of the line, you had to stand or sit on the stairs for the duration of the trip. Standing in a storm was a problem, so most often I sat on the stairs. One ferry did have handrails along the ceiling just like in the NY subway, to support you when the weather was rough.

Well, if you hadn't figured it out by now, this commuting to the mainland wasn't the best way to live. It produced stresses and unreliability that I did not want in my life. Quitting in the city and trying to find work on the island seemed like a better idea. Work was difficult to find, but as the city dwellers began to reside in the new found "burbs" of the island, there was a little more work. Also we had a great deal of tourism as time progressed. Summers were easier to find work. Year around work was hard to come by as was full time employment.

At one time I worked the days at the local food co-op until early afternoon when I moved to the local Italian restaurant to cook weekend dinners until 7 when things seriously slowed. Then off to take tickets at the local movie house where I worked for 29 years before retiring. Apparently there had been a couple who were visiting the island whom had been to each of these locations. I cashiered their order at the food co-op. I sautéed their dinner at the Italian restaurant and they saw me through the open kitchen door. When they arrived at the movies they purchased their tickets from me and asked if I had a clone working on the island as well. What are the chances of the same person serving you in three locations on the same day? Well on Whidbey during the 70's, pretty good.

Farmer's markets have become popular here on the island now that there are less farmers and more commuters. When I worked at the farmer's market there was only one. Now on the south end of the island alone there are five markets each week during the summer. Some people go to just the one that is their favorite. Others just go to the market which is first in the week. The last of the week market is probably the most traditional in the sense that it is primarily garden produce, organic and fresh, and run by the Tilth organization, an American nonprofit membership organization dedicated to supporting and advocating organic food and farming. The outdoor, seasonal markets tend to offer crafts, toys and the like, more akin to a street fair, than a farmer's market.

For about 10 years, I was the "pie lady" at the market selling about 20 to 25 pies on Saturday mornings at the market sponsored by the Tilth organization. I also sold warm muffins with butter as a snack for walking around while shopping. The Tilth organization sold coffee and had a monopoly on that. In later years I also sold mussel soup, Whidbey being world-famous for its Penn Cove mussels. This pursuit brought in a substantial income, but required that I work like crazy on Friday and Saturday and then I could rest up the rest of the week.

I am still working three days a week plus painting and writing in my "spare" time and it seems to be very spare. I tend a very large vegetable garden in the summer, and do 101 things in addition, and my so-called retirement will probably not happen until I am so grizzled and stove up that I can't drive or move around. Now I teach retirees how to paint in their leisure years. Some come to me without a clue what they will do after years of working. Many go on to be full-time painters having shows and participating in group sales and some going on to teach as well.

Working on the island is still a full time job for me and means that I wear more than three hats these days. It is probably the busiest and best time of my life. But....working in rural America certainly requires creativity.

Molly's Produce—Painting by D. Matzen

CHAPTER 11

The Public Market

"Onions can make you cry, but there has never been a vegetable that can make you laugh."—Will Rogers

I think the first time I visited Pike Place Market in Seattle was in the mid-fifties, maybe as early as 1953. It has gone through many changes in the years I have been going there. Once it was a place that solely sold fruits and vegetables raised in the local area, primarily in the truck gardens of the Kent valley south of Seattle. Now it is the hub of crafters, musicians, tony restaurants, and flying fish. The truck gardens of the Kent valley have become industrial parks.

When it began in 1907, it appeared much like the farmer's markets of today. Three square blocks of the lower downtown were dedicated to truck farmers who brought their goods to sell. Now it is the longest continuous market operating in the United States. It is also Seattle's number one tourist spot with ten million visitors a year. Quite a feat for a farmer's market. If you want to have elbow room go early in the day when the chefs from the local restaurants are checking out the goods. The crafters may not be in place that early, but the food related goods are.

The aisles of the market cover many blocks of lower Seattle still, just a few streets uphill from the Seattle waterfront. Now when I walk through this I see the fresh produce has been mostly replaced with more modern offerings. Fresh flowers abound with monstrous bouquets selling for $5 to $15. My last stop before returning to the car is to purchase one of these gigantic bouquets. Some of my favorite restaurants feature Greek, Indian, Thai, Italian, Cuban, Moroccan, Chinese, Philippine, Russian, to name some of the less unusual. Donut bars, nut bars, cheese sampling bars, sausage sampling bars, French, Russian and Chinese bakeries, dried fruits and vegetables, small-batch pickle manufacturer, beer brewing facilities and much more are additional options. There are also a number of markets that feature seafood including salmon, sturgeon, crab, shrimp (as big as lobsters), lobster, shellfish, octopus, and other specialty seafoods. As I walk down the aisles, I will try to avoid stepping in the streams of water which come from the ice melting on mountains of seafood. Piles of crab higher than my head in colorful oranges and reds. Salmon three feet long are on display. Pink and purple octopus with their circular suckers are tied in knots in piles at the fish markets. Needless to say I can smell the odor of fish and seafood with an underlying scent of flowers, flowers by the thousands, ready to be made into a special custom bouquet or chosen from the hundreds of ready-made bouquets which wait on each side of the aisle. In the fall they had one “flower” which piqued my interest. I couldn’t identify it and so I purchased a large bouquet with about a half dozen of these. They turned out to be a variety of small flowering kale that has many of these rosettes on each stock in lush lilac, turquoise, chartreuse and pale pink, yellow, and white. Really interesting and they last a long time as a cut flower. These are mixed in with color coordinated mixed blossom which enhance the kale. The whole place is a dizzying array of carnival colors and full of hectic activity and noise.

Much of the noise is melodic to some extent. About every 40 feet along the sidewalks and in the streets, and on the landings of the stairways, there are street musicians. One man brings his spinet piano five days a week and plays his own compositions. He has been doing this for about forty years. He and the piano are a little worse for wear, but he plays lively boogie-woogie which I love. Four black Americans sing Mills Brothers style next to the Russian Bakery. It must make their stomachs growl all day. There is usually a guitarist or violinist in the place of prominence next to Rachel the Pig, Georgia Gerber’s famous life-sized piggy bank where you can contribute to the maintenance of the market, or climb up on her back for your picture. The cacophony of all these street musicians in such close proximity to one another makes for an unusual syncopation, and some noise too.

Hawkers add to the circus-like quality of the environs. Buy their fish, taste the peaches (but don’t squeeze), and more. The flying fish always draw a big crowd and cause a traffic jam of folks in the already crowded aisles. This is a famous attraction where the fishmonger throws a two foot long salmon over the counter to his cohort standing amongst the crowd to the hollering of both and the screams of the onlookers. Look out, you may get sprayed with fish juice and scales. I think they use the same fish over and over throughout the day as it must do something to damage the quality of the flesh. The help probably take it home for dinner.

I always go to the alley below the market to check out the progress of the gum wall. This is a Mecca for gum chewers. I can smell the Juicy Fruit and Bazooka Bubble gum a hundred feet away. It is a brick paved narrow slot that originally was used for deliveries, but is now pedestrian only. I guess someone started sticking gum on the wall and it has become a Seattle pastime. Does any other place have a gum wall? It is colorful to say the least. Aromatic too. Knobby and pocked, colored with blue, pink, grey and more. People stand there and chew up a wad and stick it on, chew up another and stick that on. It still had its flavor, and aroma, thus the fragrance of gum all up and down the alley, sort of the smell of an old-time candy shop.

Unfortunately, recently, I was looking for small cucumbers to make garlic dills. "Unfortunate" because there are very few vegetable and fruit vendors now at the market. Most of these sell goods that are shipped in from the same places used by the local groceries and purchased from the same distributors. We used to purchase 10 pounds of these little green wonders in the '50s and '60s to make our favorite garlic dills. None of the little green garden market stands remain today. Occasionally you will find some Vietnamese farmers selling there, but alas only the tough-skinned monster cucumbers were available at the market yesterday. Most grow this bitter but pretty variety because they are noted for their tough skins which ship well and look good in the grocery store. No wonder we peel cucumbers. Perhaps the local farmers markets in the small neighborhoods have taken over the locally grown title.

Some of my fondest memories were of my trips to the market. As a young woman, recently graduated and newly hired working in downtown Seattle, for a splurge I would hoof it to the market quickly on pay day to have a lunch at the Athenian Cafe, now called the Athenian Seafood Restaurant and Grill, a three-storied Greek restaurant in the middle of the market and still there 45 years later (though the food isn't as wonderful now). I would always have the Athenian steak which came with golden, crispy hashbrowns and a Greek salad. Heaven! The steak was cut with the grain and marinated, grilled very quickly and the closest thing I had had to the steak I used to eat when I was in Mexico. It was also cheap, which was good because I made very little and this was the only occasion each month I could have beef.

Some trips to the market in the '50s included a trip to the Van de Kamp day old bakery nearby. One such trip was made with the neighbor in the summer when we were all out of school. The neighbor had 8 children. My mother, sister and I piled into their station wagon and off to buy bread and produce at the market. Twelve of us in the car left little room for purchased goods. Thus the need for army duffle bags which could be tied to the rack on the roof for transport home the thirty miles back to where we lived.

One duffle was filled with assorted breads, buns, sweet delights. In season, we could purchase hot cross buns and this was a special treat we always looked for during Lent when they are available. Now I make them myself and we can have them year-round. The other duffle was filled with produce, fish, and meat. Meat included one of our family favorites, lambs tongues from the then called Sanitary Market which was across the street from the L- shaped Pike Place Market. There was a Moroccan market that carried these delicacies and we always wanted some for dinner. I can still purchase them in the market, but now from a different vendor who specializes in serving the ethnic meat connoisseur. He also carries sweetbreads which are generally hard to find and another favorite of mine.

As we are wandering though the market, the neighbor notices she has lost one of her eight children. There is no panic as this is the ‘50s and child snatching isn’t common. So we backtrack though the market trying to find the youngest who has fallen out of step with the rest of us.

Walking back about half a block, we spy him by the fish stand where we just purchased sturgeon steaks. He is crouched down, his face looking upward under one of the big racks of fish covered in ice. It looks as though he is eyeing the structure from underneath. His mom says to him “What are you doing?” He replies, “I’m getting a drink.” “A drink?” his mom says, flabbergasted. “I’m thirsty.” It seems he is under the large table of fish with his mouth turned up to catch the drips of water coming out of the table drain from the melting ice. Well, he was probably the most inventive one amongst the bunch of us. Off we went to find refreshment for us all, we were ALL thirsty, but trained not to whine or we couldn’t make the trip next time.

In the ‘60s there was a wonderful used bookstore in the market. I could have spent days in there. It burned in a fire and was never replaced. Sad. That wing of the market is now craft stands.

Some years ago when we went to the market in the off season, and before its refurbishment, half the market was empty with the concrete display tables vacant as it wasn’t the season for much local produce. Now farmer’s markets are open year-round with greenhouse crops, winter cole crops(cabbage and broccoli family), etc. Pike Place Market is busy year-round now too, but over half of it is not green goods.

The Market Spice Store is a long-term survivor. I used to purchase Market Spice Tea there in the ‘60s. It was a heavily fragranced tea blending cinnamon, orange, allspice, clove and other spices into a tongue-numbing blend that made a better potpourri than tea. The shop still remains and sells almost any spice you can imagine even the more obscure favorites of the modernist cuisine.

Of course the market trip wouldn't be complete without a trip to DeLaurenti's. This Italian market used to be in the basement, which is now called the lower level. Now this grocer is in a place of prominence near the entrance to the market. It has everything you need that is Italian food related. I purchase wonderful cheeses from all over the world, Italian meats such as coppa and cappicola which are VERY spicy. They have an amazing selection of olive oil and occasionally host tastings. Now there is also an espresso bar and a panini station. The wine selection is extensive and one of the few places where I have a choice of several brands of vinsanto, not just one. It is not cheap.

In the '70s, I would always make a trip to DeLaurenti's in September to purchase candied fruits. They had bulk bins with halves of all the candied fruits I liked to use in fruitcakes. One year I used citron halves filled with the batter and baked. That made small, unusual fruitcakes. I would start making fruitcakes which were almost entirely candied fruit and nuts with very little batter, just enough to hold them together. These would be wrapped in muslin, which was soaked in whiskey and rewet periodically until it was time for the holidays. When the cakes were cut, they appeared jewel-like, similar to stained glass windows with the big chunks of candied fruit. They were almost too beautiful to eat.

My tastes have changed with time and my budget has changed also. Yesterday, while at the market, I dined on rough paté with dried apricots and dried sour cherries, accompanied by small cornichon, two kinds of mustard, mixed pickled vegetables and local crusty bread. A glass of merlot champagne went very well while I sketched the new Ferris wheel and the Duwamish Docks. I also sketched the other patrons, unbeknownst to them. I topped off lunch with a shot of espresso and the dessert sampler which included flourless chocolate cake with coconut whipped cream, profiteroles with vanilla gelato (which I scooped out and put in the espresso), chocolate chip bread pudding with crème anglaise, and espresso crème brulée. How's that for eating high on the hog!

Earlier in the morning I had made a trip to the Crumpet Shop for coffee and a crumpet with marmalade, which I ate while watching the baker through a glass partition as he made several hundred more on his griddle within a couple of feet of my table. The fresh baking, yeasty smell, with the steaming windows was exquisite. Wow, sensory overload. This place even has Marmite which is good for you but is on a par with cod liver oil. It definitely is a developed taste mostly by those living in British Commonwealth countries.

Later I went to the Chinese herbalist and bought some scented oils, to the Spanish Table for a good bottle of port and the Paris Grocery for duck mousse paté with port. I bought one of the $5 monster bouquets with pink lilies, pink and white dahlias, pink zinnias, and blue dried flowers. Also picked up two magazines at the great news stand at the entrance to the market which carries magazines of all genre from all over the world.

These days I lead group travel trips to interesting places with a busload of senior citizens. Twice this summer the destination was the market. They went their merry way when we arrived and we all met back at a specified site for the return to the bus and home. They had wonderful tales to share on the trip home as well. For one it was her first time to the market and to Seattle. She was overwhelmed. Since she had tired quickly and there are few places to sit and rest, she had had a progressive lunch, sampling several small dishes at 3 or 4 restaurants with the added benefit of sitting and resting. What a great idea!

The market can be a little daunting to someone who has never been there before. There is so much to see that it would take a couple of days to see it all. Tourists from out of town tend to stick to the main level on Pike Place. Many don't make it across the street to the Sanitary Market. My advice to the novice would be walk from one end to the other on the main level and mosey back slowly stopping at places which were of interest on the quick trip through. It is important to remember that there are few places to sit, so schedule an espresso and croissant at La Panier, or a crumpet at The Crumpet Shop on First Street. Lunch at one of the many ethnic choices, preferably with a view of the busy waterfront. In the late afternoon, if you are dining late that evening, stop and have a beer and do a sausage sampling at Uli's in the center of the market. As a poor shopper for anything but food, the market is about food for me. I plan meals around the wonders I find there on each trip. I go with an open mind hoping to find inspiration from the goods on hand, be it a gumbo, sweetbreads financier, veal scaloppini with fresh morels, white donut peaches soaked in vinsanto. I am bound to find something that strikes my fancy as dinner.

Though the market is not the place of my childhood, and what places have stayed the same for 60 years, I still find it a treasure trove of delights. It is definitely more crowded, has less farm produce, is missing a wonderful bookstore, but it has different and just-as-interesting sites to behold and certainly a much broader range of cuisine than it did when I was a kid. We wouldn't take 10 children in tow to such a place as we probably would lose half of them over the course of the first hour, but it is a great place to take kids who stay close to mom.

Shy one—Painting by D. Matzen

CHAPTER 12

Farm Animals—ourselves included

"Farmer, a person outstanding in their field."—D. Matzen

When my family moved to the farm, it was five acres near Redmond, Washington, a town of about seven hundred people. We moved there in 1953; I was nine year old. Most of the area was rural and used as small farm holdings, small dairy farms, truck gardens and some larger commercial farms (40 acres of broccoli next door). Of course, we wanted to do all the things that folks do when they move to a farm for the first time. My dad had grown up on a farm, but Sis, Mom and I were city girls.

Dad grew up on a farm in Valley, Nebraska, near Lincoln, where his family grew corn, watermelons, and turkeys in large amounts for sale and pork, beef and chickens for their own table. They also had milk cows with milk for sale. My mom had grown up in a city in southern California and was a city girl through and through. I had always lived with my family in towns, but, whenever space allowed we had a small vegetable patch. When we bought the farm in the summer, it already had a monstrous vegetable garden producing a LOT of food.

For some reason I don't remember, we didn't move to the farm right away. Probably painting and wallpapering (something we did a lot) to make the old house fresh for our move. We were going to move during my Christmas break at school (my sis hadn't started school yet) when all the freshening was finished.

That summer and fall I can remember picking lots of vegetables and raspberries from the new garden and taking them back to our house in the suburbs. My sis and I would take a wagon filled with lettuce, cucumbers, celery, beans, carrots, beets, turnips, parsnips, tomatoes, and more around to the neighbors to sell. The neighbors thought it was wonderful. There were no farmer's markets then. We fancied ourselves as great entrepreneurs. Why would anyone plant a fifty foot row of celery? What do you do with it? I suppose it will keep for some time, but not all winter. I certainly wouldn't can or freeze it. Selling seemed the only option.

Of course moving to the farm meant farm animals. We had our share over the years, chickens, cows, horses, pigs, dogs, cats, rabbits. Some were tried and discarded, others stayed with us until we no longer had a farm.

Chickens

The chickens were our first "farm animals." After we finally moved in and got settled, some friends who lived in Seattle decided the chickens they had been raising in their basement were outgrowing their space and needed to find a new home. Where else would they go but to our farm? So we inherited a motley crew of mixed chickens, mostly bantams (a small, pesky, independent kind of chicken), about ten as I recall. Bantams are feisty as roosters and broody as hens. Egg production is spotty when the eggs arrive at all, and are small. Mostly they didn't arrive at all.

One reason they didn't arrive was bantams like to hatch their eggs (broodiness) rather than have humans eat them. Since our chickens wandered all over the countryside, they were always off laying eggs where they wanted--often times in a blackberry patch--rather than where we wanted.

The trick here is to watch the hens for most of the day and follow the ones who have wandered off so you can locate their hidden nests, which will usually hold at least a dozen eggs. If hens haven't started to brood (set) the eggs yet and the days aren't too warm, the eggs will still be viable. If it is a hot summer, chances are the eggs aren't good, which meant that each has to be cracked into a bowl separately before being added to whatever you are cooking to prevent ruining the whole mixture with one bad egg.

One scrawny yellow-orange rooster had a bad habit of pecking. Mostly he pecked our ankles. Having rather sharp beaks, chickens can take a nice chunk of skin if they like. This became such a problem that we decided that Punkin—named for his color--should go into the stew pot. I can safely say that no amount of stewing or pressure cooking would have redeemed Punkin as a dinner. The meat was as stringy as hemp rope even after a bout in the pressure cooker. We ended up having sandwiches and tossing the stew.

One of the chores that fell to me was closing the chicken house at night to deter predators from eating the chickens, though I'm not even sure they could have chewed the stringy things! Sometimes I forgot this chore until it was dark, and thus needed a flashlight to get to the coop, which was behind the barn some distance from the house and garden. On one such late-night trip, I saw some eyes shining back toward me in the light of the flashlight. It was probably the barn cat, but as I got closer, I realized that we didn't have a black and white cat. Uh oh! A skunk! I took off lickety-split back to the house. That night my dad closed the chickens. He didn't take the shotgun because shooting a skunk can be worse than not. Making his way out to the henhouse, he just made lots of noise, and the skunk scurried off before Dad got there.

Pheasants and Chukkars

One summer when I was in high school, my dad was mowing one of the fields. He stopped and walked up to the house with three small round eggs, somewhere between the color of celadon and khaki, about the size and shape of a ping pong ball. He had uncovered a pheasant nest. The mom had taken off as he approached, her nest being hidden in the grass he was mowing.

My sis and I rigged up a plastic bucket with a towel in the bottom. We hung an electric light into the bucket and put in a thermometer. We needed to keep the temperature about 101. Since the moms perspire while they are broody, we located a spray bottle to increase the humidity in our new incubator. Once the right temperature was achieved we put in the eggs. Incubation seems as though it would be pretty simple, but a lot of things have to be right, eggs need to be turned once a day, the humidity needs to be maintained as well as the temperature. Well, it all worked out. In about two weeks we had babies. Normally it would take about 28 days, but the mom had done part of the work.

As they grew, it was evident that we had a male and two females. Male pheasants have beautiful plumage and he was a wonder to behold. The females are brown. Well for all our care and attention, the rooster turned out to be one of the meanest animals I have ever seen. Not only did he remove chunks of skin when he pecked, but he had some very glamorous scimitars to rake us up and down. Scimitars are a bony claw-like protrusion at the back of the leg just above the foot. These are a weapon that is used to fight of predators and other male pheasants who may stray into their territory.

Since he wasn't going to get any friendlier, we decided that we would return the trio to the wild. Not even a word of thanks, just off into the deep grass never to be seen again. I think that is probably where they should have been. It was a wonderful learning experience and one I have used to incubate chicken eggs a few times over the years. Now I just buy the chicks.

We also had Chukkars that we raised with the pheasants. We ate a few, but they were just a small sideline. We had received eggs from friends who raised them in California and we took two dozen to the hatchery to hatch for us. They are beautiful birds, larger and with more colorful markings than quail. We ate a few, but eventually turned them loose with the pheasants.

I did raise Chukkars again, as an adult. We ate them, but the taste of the ones we bought as chicks from the hatchery were too inbred and had no dark meat. In short they tasted just like Cornish Game Hens, so why bother?

Sheep

We never raised sheep, but our next door neighbors did. They also had a Shetland pony, but not much else. It was a large family with six children. The mom was from England and the dad was our dentist. He was a great dentist.

If you have read about our dogs you will have read about the demise of one of the sheep with our dog creating such havoc with the sheep that it had to be put down. My dad put down both the sheep and our dog. The dentist just couldn't do it.

In the U. S. sheep normally have their tails docked. This can be accomplished with a very tight rubber band or just by cutting it off. Breeding is easier if the ewe (female sheep for the unschooled) doesn't have a large, fat, wooly tail in the way. It also reduces the frequency of fly strike, a terrible problem for farmers.

Over a few years, the neighbor's tailess sheep had offspring. One was a ewe and when the time came to breed her, there were difficulties. The young ewe simply wouldn't "take." The dentist wondered if she was barren, but my dad mentioned that having a big fat tail sometimes interfered with the whole process.

Then off with the tail! The dentist figured he was a dentist and had access to Novocain, sterile equipment, and had done oral surgery, how hard could it be to cut off the tail?

Shaving the surgery area came first along with sterilizing the skin. A few shots of Novocain and he was ready. Was the ewe ready? Definitely not!

Lots of bellowing ensued, both from the sheep and the dentist. Frustration set in almost immediately when it was realized that the diameter of the bone was great and it was difficult to find a joint where he could cut. Besides that it was a bloody mess. My dad responded to the dentist's calls for help. Dad just shook his head. By this time the ewe is lying down panting and in acute distress.

How to resolve the problem? Call Doc Nichols, the vet. Doc Nichols to the rescue. He finished the surgery, wrapped the blunt end to avoid feces and infection and advised that the dentist wait until next year to breed the young ewe with the comment that the ligature method was clean, efficient and much easier on the animal. Next time use it.

The next year the young ewe had twins and they were staying in the barn. They had their tails treated and were ready to carry on. Unfortunately, two German shepherd dogs got into the barn. When the dentist heard the disturbance, he raced out to the barn to find three dead sheep and two tormenting dogs. Back to the house and out with the shotgun.

He called the neighbor who owned the dogs.

"Your dogs attacked my sheep!" said the dentist.

"They couldn't be mine, they would never do that!" said the neighbor. "You must be mistaken."

"Well, I am sorry to have disturbed you since they aren't yours. Do you know who I should call to pick up their dead dogs?"

Life on the farm.

Cows

Many of the small farms around us had dairy cattle. This was before the age of milking machines and a time when the cans of milk were left at the end of the driveway by the mailbox for a tanker truck to dump into the tank and take to the Happy Valley Dairy and Ice Cream Company in the local town. Most of these farmers lived on stump farms. If you logged the trees on your property to create pasture, but didn't remove the stumps you would still be taxed as forest land for ten years. Forest land was cheaper than pasture land. (Painted fences were taxed, but unpainted were not.) Farmers gradually rid themselves of stumps by burning garbage around a stump until it was gone. The cows liked to rub themselves on these burned stumps and frequently looked as though painted in "blackface."

Since cows were milked by hand twice a day, dairies in our neighborhood were limited in size to the amount of labor they had available. If you had lots of kids, you could have more cows as you had more hands to help with milking. Most farms had about 10-12 cows. In order for cows to produce milk, they must have calves periodically or they will go dry. Thus calves were born to about half the herd each year and a percentage of those were male and unnecessary. You could buy one of these males for $5. Holsteins were the most common type. Every other year we got one of these from some friends and raised it about 20-24 months to eat. This was usually my project. Holsteins are not efficient meat producers as the breed has a high bone to meat ratio, but they were cheap. They were also young having been taken from their moms within a couple of days of birth which necessitated bottle feeding them. In our case we used a nipple pail. This is a big galvanized bucket with a six inch rubber nipple on the lower side. Special powdered milk (baby cow formula) was mixed with warm water and the calf "nursed" on this pail making loud slurping noises until it was empty, then butting the pail until it fell off its bracket on the wall with a loud clang when hitting the floor, at which time it was time to retrieve it. By this time the bucket nipple was covered with slimy milk foam and the calf had a very foamy moostache too. Because they were destined to be another dish on our dinner table, we chose not become too attached to these animals .

Pigs

The year I was in sixth grade, my sister and I each got a weaner (just weaned) piglet, a gilt (a young female pig for you city folks). The idea was to raise the little thing up, breed it and make enough to go to college from selling the offspring. Pigs squeal a lot and we named ours Lucy and Margie after I Love Lucy and My Little Margie of '50s TV fame, where the women characters' laughter rather resembled the sound squealing pigs make.

The little critters became big, round, pink hogs weighing about 350 pounds. When they were old enough, we had the pig man bring his boar to the farm. The boar was very docile and could be handled with a crook. Our sows were also docile, so much so that we often rode around on their backs. The deed was done and the pigs were pregnant. The time from "doing the deed" to farrowing is approximately one hundred and fourteen days, almost four months. Farrowing time is birthing time in pig talk. Now folks think modern farrowing practices are inhumane. What they don't understand is that every time the mother has a baby, she stands up to look at it and if left unattended in a large space, will step on the little one and kill or injure it. Thus the sow is confined. When the piglet is born, it is removed. Its needle-like teeth clipped and then placed under a heat lamp with its sibs until all are born (my job and one for which I stayed home from school, twice). Then all the squirming, pink, little piglets are put together when mom is in a better mood and can focus on her babies instead of contractions. Massive mealtime.

My pig had fifteen babies and my sis's had fourteen. Now we were in the pig business in a big way. Twenty-nine little pink sausages. Piglets can walk, squeal, and run practically from the get go. We turned them loose in the pig pen, a largish affair behind the barn. Unfortunately the fence was to keep in the big pigs, not the little ones. They ran all over hill, dale and the pastures just like a flock of birds startling the horse and the cows. Since they were a very light pink, almost white, they were easy to see as they galloped across the fields. They could change direction in unison going full tilt. It was pretty amazing to watch. When they got hungry, they all raced back to mama. If they were all sleeping in a pig pile and one got up for a snack, it was a mad dash to mama so no one had more than the rest.

(notice Mom and Sis looking out the barn window)

When the pigs were about ten weeks old, my dad and I castrated the males. Sounds terrible; and it was done without benefit of any medication except mercurochrome. The little fellows screamed louder than ever and had very rosy butts from the mercurochrome swabs for several days. When it was time to wean the little ones (weaner pigs), we separated them from their moms and there was quite a bit of anxiety. No more lunch on mom, now they had to fend for themselves at the trough. We fed them a special meal from feed yard materials and leftovers and scraps from the kitchen.

Soon it was time to sell them as we were not equipped to raise that many pigs to adulthood. Unfortunately, between breeding time and weaner pig sale time, the market on pork had collapsed. We advertised at the feed store and in the local eight page newspaper and by word of mouth. Trying to sell twenty-eight (one had startled the horse and received a deadly kick) was impossible. We dropped the price to $5 each and still couldn't sell them.

We were small time farmers and did not have room to house that many pigs nor could we afford to feed them up to butchering size. I think we probably sold three or four. I remember when the folks came to get them, the little critters decided to go on walkabout in the woods. We chased piglets everywhere, finally getting a couple for them to take home. Lots of bramble wounds and nettle stings to tend to after they left.

What were we to do with all these pigs? The only viable solution was to eat them ourselves. Dad and I butchered them all, cleaned, gutted, and scraped off their bristle hair. He had bought something called butcher's wax which was a bilious yellow and similar to cheese wax (it may possibly have been cheese wax). We heated this sticky wax and dipped each cleaned little porker in it, coating it thoroughly. We stacked them up like cordwood in the upright freezer and ate roast suckling pig several times a month. We invited all sorts of people to share in this exotic cuisine which for us was everyday fare.

I didn't go to college on the money I made raising pigs, but I must say I got an education in the process.

Horses

Every small girl's dream is to have a horse. Perfectly natural, especially when you have moved to a small farm. It took my sis and me a couple of years to save the money, but we finally had enough. We went to north Seattle, the region that is now Aurora Village, a large shopping mall. There was a horse trader there: he also rented pack horses to hunters and folks who hiked the mountains on horses. My sis and I had our silver dollar collection in our pockets. We talked with the man and handed over seventy-five silver dollars to pay for Lady Jane Grey as we named her. Lady for short. She was our main ride for many years and a wonderful, gentle, dappled grey horse. We got her home and climbed onto her bareback not being able to afford a saddle as well as a horse. She started trotting and we promptly fell off. We had no knowledge of squeezing with our knees to stay on the horse. Later we saved enough to purchase a saddle too.

Lady had a previous life of which we were unaware. She had been a cattle cutting horse. She was accustomed to cutting cattle, her job was to separate out parts of a herd. Our five Herefords were herded from one corner of the pasture to the other constantly. They were losing weight. We finally had to put Lady in a separate pasture to stop her from her favorite sport, herding.

My mother, the city girl, had never ridden a horse, nor did she have the desire to ride a horse, but Dad and my sister and I talked her into her one and only ride. Mom came out to the back pasture to tell us lunch was ready and we talked her into getting on the saddled horse (with horn to hang onto) and riding her back to the barn. Lady knew there was a novice on board and decided to act up. She took off at a gallop, with my mother barely able to hang on and with no instruction on how to use reins. I'm not even sure she was holding the reins she had such a tight grip on the horn. Off they went, lickity split, headed for the barn. Our barn door was a wide opening, about ten feet, but it lacked height. My sis and I would bend over the horse's back to get into the barn without disembarking. My mother, however, was more concerned about staying on and didn't see the low entry. Lady scraped Mom off neatly into the barnyard muck. Mom's only injuries were to her pride, but her anger was unmatched for many a day.

After Lady passed on, we found another horse, a beautiful palomino named Avalanche. He lived on the Carnation Dairy Farm in Carnation, Washington. This was the farm where Carnation Feed Company tested food products for various animals, dogs, cats, sheep, cows, horses, etc. The manager lived on the farm and his daughter had a horse. She had gone to college and the horse was just getting fat and ornery in the pasture. They would sell him for a good price. He was beautiful, but he wouldn't go into the horse trailer to come to our house. Several farm hands tried every trick in the book, but the horse wouldn't go in the trailer. We went home without the horse.

A week later, my family and I went back to the farm with the bicycle in the back of the truck, minus the trailer. My dad and I took turns riding Avalanche home the twenty miles to our house. Needless to say the horse wasn't so ornery after that trip. My dad was a little sore because he hadn't ridden a horse or a bicycle that much or that far in any recent time.

Farm Dogs

No farm is a farm without a farm dog. Farm dogs on the farm have many duties, one of which is to ward off predators. Skunks were the only predators we really had to worry about back then, since skunks are both chicken and egg-eaters. It was the skunk's defense mechanisms that were most worrisome. Luckily we never had a dog get mixed up with skunk. The dogs would bark, but stay well out of range.

Penny was our first farm dog, the color of the copper of a not-so-shiny penny. She was a beauty and a pure bred. Not your typical farm dog mutt. She was a German shorthair pointer. She was supposed to be a hunting dog. We had lots of pheasants around the neighborhood then and my dad liked to hunt. He sometimes went to Eastern Washington bird hunting. Shorthairs are bird dogs. One of their main jobs is to point up birds hiding in the grass and scare them up for the hunter. Bird dogs are supposed to have a soft mouth. This means that the dog will not damage the bird when she retrieves it. Penny would catch a chicken and it around in her mouth until you took it away from her. Sometimes it would be hours that she carried it around. The chicken, looking stricken, but unhurt, would be soaking wet from Penny's saliva. When you finally saw that she had a chicken you would tell her "good girl" and Penny would drop it at your feet. The chicken, somewhat the worse for wear would lay on the ground for a few seconds before standing, stand shaking dog spit all over us.

Finally Dad decided it was time to try his bird dog out on the pheasants. Off they went to the far back pasture to point up some birds. Penny instinctively did her job and two birds flew up just in front of her. My dad took his shot and the dog was off like a shot for the house. I had never seen her run so fast with her short little tail between her legs. She ran all the way back to the house and jumped right through the window of the mudroom door, breaking the glass and all the mullions. When we got there, she was cowering in the corner under the utility sink, shaking like a leaf. So much for bird dogging. She never went hunting again.

Over the years, we had a range of various rovers. There was the Irish terrier who we got for free because his previous owner felt he needed more exercise; this dog was just too spirited for her home and for a woman of her age. He was a scrapper. We thought he would be good to keep the coyotes away at the new house where we were living. Unfortunately he decided that the neighbor's sheep needed to be taught a lesson. Both the dog and the sheep had to be put down.

There was Charlie. He was a tan and black Border Collie. He wandered into our yard one day and made himself to home. Charlie could smile. I doubt that he scared any predators with his smile. He did, however, scare the neighbor dentist when he came over for coffee. "That dog showed me his teeth!" I said, "Maybe he knew you were a dentist. Not really," I added, "he just likes to smile." About a year later Charlie went on walkabout and never returned. When I was learning to drive I spotted a familiar-looking dog in a neighborhood about thirty miles from our home. I opened the window and said, "Hi, Charlie!" and he smiled at me.

At one time there was a large mongrel dog, Stubby Wigglebottom. He had a short tail that wiggled his whole backside. He wouldn't stay home. Since the sheep incident, we were worried about a dog that wandered. Consequently, we tied him up. He chewed a hole through the corner of the house. He was reprocessed to another household with a high fence, which probably he chewed a hole through as well.

The final dog we had on the farm was Schnitzel and you can probably guess what kind of a dog he was. Now what good is a dachshund on a farm? They are great badger hunters, but we didn't have badgers. We did have Rocky Mountain Beavers, a kind of varmint that's like a cross between a gopher and a prairie dog, and we had muskrats that burrowed in the river bank. Schnitzel found his own niche in our farm society. He felt it was his job to lick the cows' utters. Calves like to create a lot of milk foam when they nurse, and much of that foam remains on the udder. When the cow would lie down, Schnitzel ran out to the field and cleaned her udder of any remaining foam. The cows didn't mind.

Farming as an Adult

To this day I still raise chickens for eggs, however, I have purchased a more efficient egg machine than the old bantams we had when I was young. I sell the surplus eggs and occasionally we eat an old hen. Nowadays you cannot seem to find stewing hens in the market. I really like them for fricassee and chicken and dumplings. So when a hen is past her laying prime, she can be fattened up and stewed. No waste here.

My hens are confined to their hen run most of the time. It is fairly large and I throw all my weeding materials and trimmings to them often. I feed them sprouted wheat grass and many days old bread from the bakery (organic, of course). I grow the wheat grass in my greenhouse on a nine day cycle. Eight pie tins with holes in the bottom in which the wheat sprouts. I soak the wheat seeds overnight and then pour them into the pie tin each morning. With eight tins I have 2-3" high sprouted wheat with the seeds attached to feed them in nine days, start to finish. I also let them into the vegetable garden in the winter to clean up the weed seeds and eat the bugs....no way is a chicken a vegetarian! I have to laugh at the store bought eggs that say "From organic, free range, vegetarian chickens." There is no such thing. Chickens will eat anything. They are also diggers. They can dig up a row of newly emerged beet plants in about fifteen minutes. They are particularly fond of the bedding plants you just set out in the flower patch. It is easy to do away with an old hen that has just eaten $20 worth of bedding plants. They are good at turning over soil if you have an area that needs a good work over.

In more recent times, we had a big bird living with us. A BIG BIRD. For a long time I didn't name her. A peahen who adopted us, she was the female form of peacock. One day two of them were wondering around our yard. If you never have been close to one, they seem very large. They also tend to wander. We have had them in the neighborhood before. One chased my dachshund around the yard years ago. Several roosted on the peak of our house back then too.

Several weeks later there was only one peahen present in the yard. She would show up every morning when I went out to feed the chickens. I supposed that she needed access to water so I put out a pan of water for her. I didn't think that she would stay around. She disappeared every day after our short visit in the morning. Finally I watched her, reminiscent of those banties who would wander off after feed time and sure enough, she had a nest at the end of our bocce court. Her egg hatched, but we never saw the baby. I still have the shell in a bird's nest on my window sill.

Six months later she was still with us. I named her finally, thinking she would probably disappear as soon as I did, but not so. We named her Penny Peahen. She liked the company of our chickens and asks to be let into their yard to eat their goodies each morning when I let the chickens out. Some mornings she was still on her roost in a tall fir tree near the henhouse. When she came sweeping down, you think you are being invaded by a pterodactyl as she was a very large, strangely shaped presence in the sky.

At sunset she flew up to her roost about 40 feet up the tree and called and called in a loud, echoing call which can travel miles. I think she would have liked to find a mate, but I doubted there were any in the region. I thought that in the spring when she would make her nest and lay her eggs (yes, female birds lay eggs without males, they just aren't viable), I would substitute some chicken eggs for hers so she could have a family. But as fate would have it, her desire to find a mate was too great and she walked off into the sunset, literally.

At one time we had a neighbor who fancied herself as a farmer on her 2 acres of land. She had two horses and three or four cows, 2 goats and a pig. There were chickens in there too. I don't know if she had housing for any of them. I do know that she didn't have much feed for them as they were always escaping to forage for food. My garden is fenced, but the old woman who lived in a ten foot trailer across the street from me couldn't afford fencing. The cows were constantly coming up to eat her vegetables. This was not a good thing as she raised almost all of her own food. We would shoo the cows back down the road, but they would break into the garden again and return almost daily. The animals owner didn't seem to think it was a problem.

One day I drove past the animal owner's house to see the goats on the roof of her house. I have no idea how they got up there. Goats are climbers, but that was something to behold. Didn't help the roofing with them scampering around on it. I don't know how she got them down.

The pig she owned was a different story. She was raising it to eat. Since she worked nights in a bar, she brought home the food wastes for the pig. There must not have been enough as the pig escaped too. Pigs are great at traveling cross-country. They don't have to stick to roads and trails like the cows. We never saw it get away and it didn't browse in our yard on the way. Pigs root. Rooting means taking their snout and digging in the dirt. They like to eat the roots of plants and trees. They are great for ridding an area of the dreaded blackberries because they kill them at the source, the roots. Their skin can be like armor making them suited for battling the invasive, viscious blackberries. They make very effective rototillers.

Well the pig was gone. One day a man from about a mile and a half down the road came through the neighborhood knocking on doors. Had we lost a pig? No we hadn't, but the lady farmer up the road had. He contacted her and told her to come get the pig. He had confined it and was feeding it until he found the owner. A month later he came by again and asked her again to come get her pig. Two months later he had the pig cut and wrapped and HE ate the pig. Not long after that the lady farmer was told by the sheriff that she would lose her animals due to neglect. She moved with all the animals in the dead of night and we never learned where she moved. I hope the animals found greener pastures.

Buying chicks. Yes you can purchase baby chicks, usually day old. We can get them at the local feed store, but the feed yard decides the breeds. The first order of chicks this year was cancelled because there was so much snow in Iowa where the feed store purchases them in bulk. They get day old ducks, poults (baby turkeys) and sometimes goslings (baby geese).

My preferred method of purchasing poultry is to order from the source. I have more choices. I read all the information such as size of eggs, color of eggs (we sell brown), size class of the bird, number of eggs per year, length of time to laying (usually in direct correlation to the size of the adult bird and up to 8 months), disposition of the bird, suitability for cold or wet or hot climate. Picking a bird that has the right characteristics will help with the success of production.

The morning the chicks hatch (21 days incubation) they are placed in a small box with sisal bedding. Minimum 25 chicks for warmth and survival. I purchase pullets (females) as I only want one rooster. I purchase a new rooster about every third batch of chicks. I order chicks every other year. The problem of hatching your own is at least half are roosters. One clutch (a group of eggs incubating) under an old broody biddy hatched all roosters! What are the chances of that happening? Pretty rare, I imagine.

The small box full of fuzzy, grey chicks is peeping away to the post office where they are sent second day air to me. Chicks have the ability to live off residual materials in their bodies which has fed them while they were incubating. They are hungry when they get here and that is a good thing.

The brooder: Mine is usually a cardboard refrigerator box with some of one side removed to reach in to see the chicks. I have a heat lamp inside the box to keep them warm with clean water and feed. I have prepared this box ahead of the ship date so it is ready and that the temperature is stable BEFORE they arrive. Very important if you want success.

The delivery: About 5 in the morning, the phone rings. Your chicks are here. I have clothes set out so I can race to the post office straight from bed. The post mistress is always in a big hurry to be relieved of this fragile shipment. I race home and out to the barn where the brooder is ready.

Last time it didn't go so smoothly. I get to the local post office and they don't know why I am pounding on the back door. I was told to come to the back door when they called earlier. The Chinese lady that works there doesn't understand what I need. I go "peep peep" and she says "no." Through a lot of transliteration and charades, I finally determine they are at a more distant post office about ten miles from my house.

Well, all is well and they are thankful to be relieved of the fragile, noisy package.

At home: I take each chick out of the box. Dip its beak in water and then into the powdery crumbles it eats. It looks at all this stuff on its face and shakes its head and then drinks a bunch of water. Once one sees another do this, it isn't long until the monkey see, monkey do system takes full affect. From then on it is keeping them in food and water. About five months later, my variety, Black Astralorps will start laying beautiful extra large brown eggs. Ah, the wonders of nature.

If I get the chicks in the spring, this means that the eggs will generally come in the fall. They will lay for a year, at which time they will molt. Molting is like teething. They get punky and use all the protein they consume to make new feathers, not eggs. We will go until probably February before we see another egg. I have tried buying chicks every year, but it is too much work, so I stockpile eggs in late summer to tide us over. We never make it the whole way to February, but at least we have homegrown eggs for a while during the molt.

Worms

Most people wouldn't consider worms livestock, but we also raise worms in worm bins. These are three fifty gallon garbage pails with small holes drilled in the bottom. I put the kitchen wastes, excluding bones, and whatever doesn't go to the chickens. That is onion skins, citrus peels, unappetizing celery stalks, potato peels and the like. I also put in shredded paper that I receive from work and from our outdated materials at home. We have thousands of worms in the three bins and give them away regularly for others to start bins as well. When we lived in Beijing I started one on the porch of our apartment in the fall so I would have some decent soil to plant pots for the following summer when I grew scarlet runner beans and flowers. One recent summer I won best worm compost of the entire county fair. It was beautiful. My little critters work well and win special awards!

Ring Necked Doves

I started with just a couple doves so I could hear them singing. We had them when I was growing up too. A large cage hung in the apple tree. Now I have a large run for them. They are happy and will let me pet them when I feed them. Just recently we had a baby hatch and he is just now learning to fly. Dove mothers feed their babies through regurgitation. When they hatch they are about the size of a peanut with no feathers. Within days they start to feather and in about a week to nine days their eyes open. From then on they are watching the world. They want to get out there and get their own food. Sometimes when they first start to eat on their own, they eat too much and die. I always feel very sad about this. We have very happy doves, that is why I have seventeen now and am selling at least a half dozen or more each year. I sold seven this spring. They were even laying eggs in December, but those weren't successful, for which I am thankful as it is hard for them to raise a baby when it is below freezing. I don't understand why they do this. Maybe because when it is cold the sun is generally shining brightly. Maybe they are light sensitive. I love to hear them cooing and singing. It is one of the best sounds on the farm.

I am now getting to an age where I wonder if having animals is the best thing, but for the time being, I will continue. They give a lot of joy and....this morning, three eggs!

Photo courtesy of Library of Congress (Middle stump a similar size to ours)

Chapter 13

It's a Blast!

Many farms had stumps which I have written about elsewhere in another chapter. We removed most of the stumps in our newly cleared fields and piled them into enormous stump piles to be burned.

My mom, the pyromaniac (a trait I must have inherited), waited until the piles were really dry and then started the fire. These were not small bonfires, but humongous piles the size of the house I now live in and larger, a real conflagration when fully burning.

On one occasion, the stump pile was particularly dry and Mom began to worry the fire might spread to the neighboring grass field. Off to get the tractor with a harrow on the back. Her intent was to plow (harrow) around the pile in several concentric circles, leaving a dirt margin wide enough to deter the spread of the fire.

In her hurry, coming from the opposite end of the field, she snagged the outflow line from the well house and as she continued across the field we tried to get her attention over the noise of the tractor engine. Oblivious to the fact that water was shooting in the air from the well head she continued to the fire.

I raced down to the well head and shut off the valve that turned off the water to the house. Water continued to drain from the house that was about twenty feet higher than the well, until all the water was gone. Now the pump would stop running full blast to try to keep up with the non-existent demand from the house.

As Mom was circumnavigating the stump pile, she noticed the commotion back at the well head. Now we had additional work to do besides protecting the spread of the fire. When Dad came home, he fixed the well head supply pipes so we would have water to clean ourselves up.

Just one of the exciting episodes working on the farm.

When the stumps were removed from the field, some of the larger cedar ones were left as the equipment used for clearing couldn't handle a stump eight feet tall, five feet in diameter and cedar, which rots very slowly. Large huckleberry bushes grew from the summit up another six or eight feet. I kind of liked these stumps which still had the springboard slots visible about five feet from the ground. The spring board fit in the slot and the sawyer stood on it to cut the stump. It was dangerous work.

Now we needed the blasting man. The blasting man, whose name I have long forgotten, was a bent, scrawny, sunburned (maybe blast burned) old man, not nearly as tall as me. He was missing several of his fingers and his fingernails were bent and broken so as to be unrecognizable. He had a great sense of humor and we always enjoyed the occasions he came to work for us.

Blasting a monster stump took lots of calculating as well as dynamite. Holes were bored around the base of the stump and dynamite was packed down these cavernous hollows. The cord to the detonator was strung across the field to a safe distance from flying debris—or so he said. How did he end up so beaten if he was always a safe distance away? This part of the process could take half a day until the long awaited moment of THE BLAST. We ran to the neighbors or called to let them know to open their windows. Sometimes the blast could blow out the windows in an enclosed building just from the percussive blast wave. Some of the neighbors came to watch. It was better than the fourth of July.

The blast would happen, and since we were a ways away, the sound didn't arrive simultaneously. Instead what we SAW was a giant red, orange and yellow column of flame skyrocket twenty to thirty feet in the air. Then the blast. Not much flying debris. The stump simply split just like orange segments and laid back in eight tidy pieces on the ground.

We all raced down to check out the results. They were similar for most of the stumps over the years, but one particularly large stump was different. When we raced down there to look into the cavern under the stump, there were dozens of garter snakes writhing about. They didn't die, but they were certainly shell shocked.

We had a small seep that ran through the low part of our property. My sis and I use to make dams with rocks to create tiny ponds and wade around in the mud and muck in the summer when it was hot. The seep usually flowed year around, but was hardly more than a wet spot most of the summer.

My dad decided a pond might be nice and he was talking to the stump blaster about how it would be nice to have a pond down by the wet part of the pasture, could the stump blaster recommend someone to dig a pond?

Dig a pond? Why he could do that for us. Easy as pie and only a day or so to create. How large did we want? Dad said sixty by a hundred would probably be nice so we could see it from the house.

The process began. Dynamite was embedded in the mud in the low area, lots of dynamite. He spent a great deal of time with it.

Word went out around the neighborhood that we were having a blasting day at our house and everyone was invited to come and watch, have cinnamon rolls, coffee, tea and entertainment after having opened their windows. We were probably five hundred feet from the blasting site.

We all got our coffee and goodies and lined up on the balcony on the upper floor of the house. We had some chairs and table as well as a chaise or two. There was the stump blaster stringing the line to the detonator so the fun was about to begin.

The blast went off and there were no heavenward flames this time. Instead there was a wall of mud and muck shooting skyward and racing in our direction. We had eaves on the house so we all turned and pressed against the house, under the eaves to protect ourselves. Well the angle of the flying mud was such that the eaves were useless and it plastered us and the house siding. When we stepped away from the house you could see each of our clean profiles clearly. Unfortunately, the backs of us were completely covered with mud. We walked around to the front of the house to a hose bib and hosed everyone down. Fresh refreshments came out from the kitchen and we all laughed and thanked our lucky starts that there were no rocks catapulted with the muck. I got the job of hosing down the house.

It took several days for the pond to fill with water, but it was a glorious site to behold. I was hoping we could plant fish, but we never did. I would occasionally eat my lunch sitting near it and enjoying having a real pond.

On another occasion, I was in college and came home to spend the weekend. I was sitting in the family room with my Mom and Dad having a conversation about events at college. We looked out the sliding glass door across the creek, road and pasture toward the neighbor's house and noticed a big fog bank approaching across the region. It was so strange that we got up to look out the window.

I wondered if the temperature was dropping and that was causing the fog bank. I opened the sliding glass door to go out. My dad started out first. The cloud was very near now, just across the creek and by the road. There were tall fir trees along part of the creek and they had become enveloped in the fog.

Suddenly there was a horrendous blast, so strong that my two hundred pound father fell back into me and my mother and into the house. The explosion was greater than any stump removal or pond making we had ever had. The sound of it left our ears ringing and we couldn't hear for a short while. It knocked the breath out of our chests. We are all sitting up on the floor of the family room having been forced back by the percussion of the blast. No one could understand what had happened.

Probably five seconds later, debris started raining down all around the house. Most of it was wood about the size of a chopstick with a few larger pieces.

When the fog moved on we could see the source of the blast. There had been a tall fir tree standing by the creek and it was now only about a third as high as previously. The top third of the tree was laying in the creek and the middle third was the chopsticks laying all over the yard. Luckily they weren't driven horizontally or my dad would have been impaled. Instead they "rained" down all around the neighborhood.

Our neighbors, about five thousand feet away had horses. They were frantic, racing around and screaming. They ran into the loafing shed and started kicking at the walls. When the neighbors came home they found chaos. The windows were broken in the house, the goods in the upper kitchen cupboards were laying on the floor. They thought they had been vandalized. When they checked on the horses they discovered the metal gate and metal fencepost had been welded together. It must have been a terrific shock for the horses as they were still fussing several hours later.

The fog bank was apparently a very low, charged cloud, not fog, though we were not located at a high elevation. The cloud enveloped the tree and grounded its electrical charge. The sap in the tree boiled, unable to release the steam and exploded in an extremely impressive manner.

My sister and brother-in-law were in the town of Bellevue, probably eleven miles away as the crow flies and they heard the blast. No wonder we couldn't hear much for a time. Dad said it was the first time he could remember that he could breathe through both nostrils at once. It cleared his head completely.

Now that WAS A BLAST!

Sis' First Day of School

CHAPTER 14

School Days

"The most important thing we learn at school is the fact that the most important things can't be learned at school." — Haruki Murikami

Moving from a fairly large suburban town to the countryside made for a few changes in my life. I was in the second half of fourth grade when we changed schools, yet again. This would be the fifth school in five grades including kindergarten. Four of these changes involved towns, or small city school districts, but this last one when we moved to the farm was a rural school. The building was an ancient two-story, dark brown brick building that smelled as antiquated as it was. Around the beginning of the 1900s it had housed all grades except kindergarten which was still not offered when we arrived. The high school had been moved to a town about ten miles distant. But the biggest changes were the students and teachers.

Most of the teachers in this district had been teaching there since the beginning of time. I was assigned to a spinster lady who was in her dotage and mean as a junkyard dog. I had never experienced such a teacher in the schools in larger towns. They had all been relatively young, progressive, somewhat permissive and good teachers. This one frowned constantly, looked for someone to punish, and told my mother she didn't want me in her class, I should be in third grade not fourth based on my age. Abilities had nothing to do with it.

I have to say, I was scared! I knew she didn't like me, seeing me as a spoiled city girl and one much younger than her classmates. There was no way I could overcome that.

So on with trying to learn. My classmates were mostly farm children with animals to tend, cows to help milk, chickens to feed, pigs to slop and little income. I hadn't acquired any animals yet when I started there, they arrived later. It was January, which may have been a reason for me to be different than everyone else. I have no idea why I wasn't started in September at the beginning of the school year. As I mentioned elsewhere, it was probably because my folks were working on modernizing and remodeling the farmhouse and we couldn't or wouldn't move in until the Christmas holidays.

Anyone who has moved as a child knows how hard it is to start fresh, knowing no one in the new class. Unsure what they are learning, and the teacher unsure of what you have learned, which in this teacher's opinion was nothing. I was quiet and made friends slowly. None of my classmates lived near where I lived and we all took the school bus as parents couldn't afford to take the time to come and get you either at school or at a friend's after school.

It was a struggle, but I worked hard to at least learn my lessons and eventually made a couple of friends by the end of the term. That summer between fourth and fifth grades the mean, old teach told my parents that she would flunk me unless I attended summer school. She mentioned that I would then be with my "proper" age group and she would have me again in fourth grade that year. I went to summer school, half day. My first summer living on the farm was spent with considerable time in the classroom. It was depressing. In fifth grade my teacher was just as old but not mean and I enjoyed that more. By then life had become somewhat normal and no longer with everything new.

High school was another challenge. By the time I started in the late ‘50s it was the overwhelming new experience all over again. Though some of my old classmates were there with me, more than half the students were from a large town where the school was located. They were the “townies” and we were the country bumpkins. I still occasionally see a man who attended this school as a townie and he still refers to me as a country bumpkin even though my father worked five days a week in Seattle and we attended events in Seattle often. Most of the classmates from the country had never been to Seattle though it was only thirty miles away. My mother was determined that we would not be bumpkins.

I went on to university and received a BFA in fine art, then to graduate school. I taught for twenty-five years. Am I still a country bumpkin? I am working hard to become that, even if the burbs have encroached to the point it seems impossible.

Summer Bouquet—Painting by D. Matzen

Chapter 15

The Admirer

"Life is the flower for which love is the honey." — Victor Hugo

I will always remember the first time someone was in love with me. It wasn't my birth and the love that parents feel when they bring their firstborn into the world. I don't remember that. I was, however, very young when it happened. It was boy in love with girl, though not reciprocated, fourth grade to be exact. I was nine years old. It was a very curious and a somewhat embarrassing experience.

I guess I don't understand what happened, but during late fourth and all through fifth grades, several of the boys fell in love with me. I have since learned that this is the new gal in town syndrome. We had moved and I had entered a new school just after Christmas break,.I was someone new and exotic. My family didn't encourage anything like boyfriends for an eight to ten year old me. It wasn't something that was acceptable in that era or in a rural community such as the one in which we lived. Even in this day and age, I still would like children to be children until they are mature enough to understand all that not being a child entails. Something that doesn't happen anyway, but we can always hope. Probably these budding romances happened because I was the new girl on the block. I guess that the boys found intrigue in the unknown. One of the potential candidates was a little mature for his age. I'm not sure that he hadn't been held back, probably a few times as he seemed to be showing a little shadow along his jaw line. He was in fourth grade too, remember?

Anyway, it now was summer. I was doing all the new things one would do when recently moved to a farm. We had gotten chickens, a new dog and we had a large vegetable garden that needed a lot of weeding. The horse and pigs were yet to come, but we did have a few cows. Most of the summer my sister and I were covered with dust and blackberry juice and scratches and debris from cleaning the chicken house. Certainly we were typical country children with dirt around our mouths and dull, dusty hair, smelling of hay and chicken yards. We were wallowing in the wonders of living on a farm and loving every minute of it. It was all new and all so wonderful.

One day, heading toward fall, but still the dog end of summer, Carolyn, a friend I had made in my new school came to our farm. She lived through the woods and down a different road from ours, about half a mile away as the crow flies. That year she was probably the only friend I had made during my short time in our new digs.

Carolyn knocked on the door and I thought she had come to play, an unusual thing considering the distance and the chores we all had to do. I was surprised. My mom was happy that I had a friend who would come to see me in our new neighborhood as Carolyn lived some distance from us.

She had come bearing a gift. It was a bottle of perfume, bright pink in color with a very elaborate pressed glass bottle faceted like a diamond, and a four inch high plastic faux jeweled finial on the top in blue plastic. It was a wonder to behold, sparkling in the sunlight. It was Apple Blossom perfume for ME! I didn't understand. She told me her cousin was in love with me and it was a gift from him. I don't think he was even in my fourth grade class, but in another teacher's class. I was astonished. I didn't know what to say. I had NEVER had a gift from a boy before. I had never had a boyfriend. I was only nine years old!

The worst part was she told me he was hiding out behind a cedar stump in the field to the south of the house. He was too shy to bring it in himself. What was I to do? We lived on a five acre farm that had two fields, a barn, some out buildings and a few large stumps too big to remove out in the south field. He stood behind one peering out.

I walked out the back door and looked to the south and waved a "thank you" to him. I am not sure he saw or even acknowledged my wave. He certainly didn't come up to the house after.

Carolyn and I had a chat about how summer was going and about the soon to arrive school term, and a short while later, she walked out into the field and the two of them wandered off to the woods from whence they came, waving good-bye and never a word was said again about the incident, even after school started again in the fall. I was a little chagrined to meet up with him during the new fall term, but I needn't have worried. He never spoke to me before or after the incident. Flummoxed would best describe my puzzlement. It was an event that really happened, but it was a mystery. Was it real? Yes, as real as the bottle that sat in my window sill and reflected its facets on the walls and ceiling of my bedroom for several years to come. Curious.

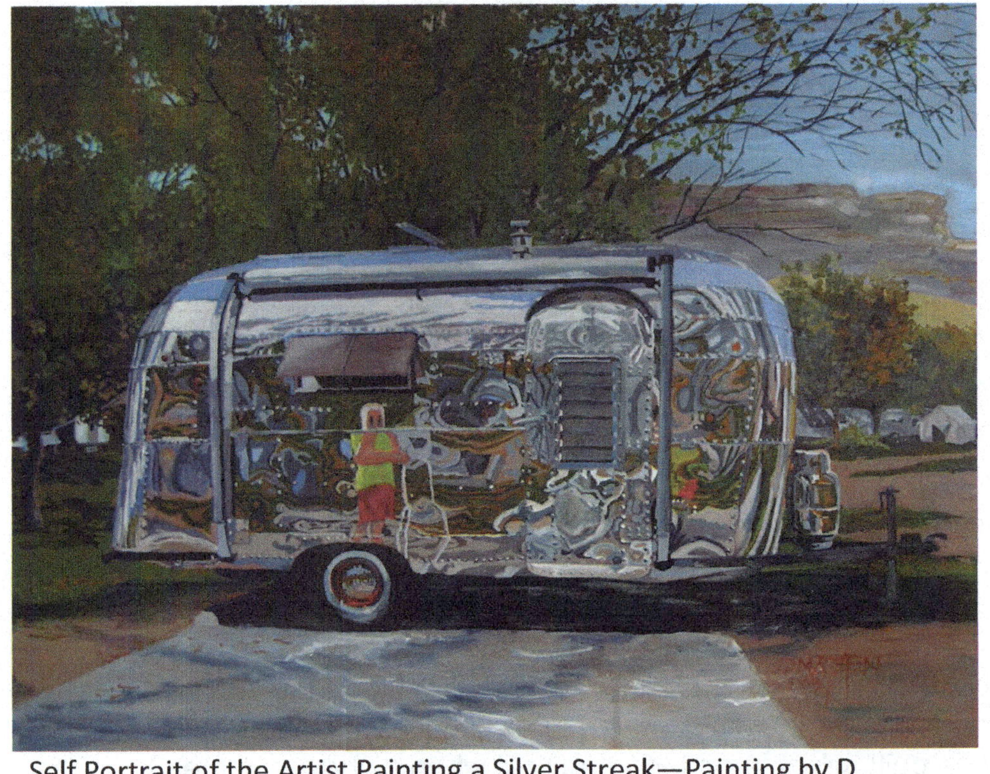

Self Portrait of the Artist Painting a Silver Streak—Painting by D. Matzen

CHAPTER 16

Sleeping Around

For my part I know nothing with any certainty, but the sight of the stars makes me dream.--Vincent Van Gogh

This is not an X rated chapter, too bad. It is suitable for children and family. It is PG.

For most of my life I have liked sleeping outdoors, not an easy feat when you live in the Puget Sound Basin of Western Washington, where it frequently rains. I did it as a child and still do it as an adult sleeping on the deck or the back patio. My longest season of sleeping outdoors came when I lived on a small farm in Redmond, Washington in the 1950s. My dad, having purchased a new canvas wall tent in hopes of encouraging my mom to participate, allowed my sis and me to spend almost five months sleeping continuously outdoors.

There are disadvantages to sleeping in a tent, and it is not my favorite choice for sleeping outdoors as I like to wake and watch the stars, but the tent allowed us to sleep out even through misty rains that are common to our area. However, if you are touching the walls of a canvas tent in the rain, you will get wet. Tents do allow for a certain amount of security and protection from the elements and critters that frequent the night.

Over the years, various varmints have found my sleeping on the ground a good place for them to keep warm. I have slept on picnic tables in campgrounds to avoid rattlesnakes crawling inside my sleeping bag. I slept on the ground for many years. I have slept in my old Volvo station wagon with the back door open so I could look out at the stars through the hatch window. Now we have a queen-sized air bed with complete bed coverings, including sheets and a handmade quilt, which aren't too practical when a shower comes through but we keep a plastic tarp under the edge of the mattress for this type of emergency. All we need to do is pull it out and cover ourselves. If it is raining too hard, we cover the bed and retreat to the house where it is dry and warm.

Well, having just moved to the farm the previous winter, the first summer after fourth grade, my sis and I wanted to try sleeping out, our first such experience ever, not just in this new and different world. It was more private than the burbs. I was nine and she was five. My dad bought us new Dacron, washable sleeping bags, a much improved and lighter weight version than the old-fashioned kapok that was previously available. Back then we didn't sleep on any padding; we just lay down on the brick patio outside the back door. It seemed very cold and hard compared to my bed in the house. It was also very dark as there were no streetlights or even a barn light. My eyes became accustomed to the darkness and I could see shapes and forms in the night, the barn, the chicken house, the dog house, though we had yet to acquire a dog. Back then, we didn't light up the countryside with outdoor lighting. I still don't, and the advantage is that one can see the stars in the sky. It took a long time for me to fall asleep that night. The newness of everything, the new and wonderful sleeping bags, being outdoors at night, seeing stars and hearing all kinds of sounds, night birds, coyotes, the horse walking around chewing grass, the chickens grumbling in the henhouse. There was a lot happening to keep me alert. I must admit, I WAS SCARED! I needn't have been because I could always run indoors and jump in my own warm bed. I fell asleep, probably a lot faster than it seemed.

Sometime in the middle of the night, I awoke. Probably not surprising because of the newness of this adventure and allowing for the fact that I was only nine years old.

What had awakened me? I lay still and listened. Something was walking across the foot of my sleeping bag and making snuffling noises. We had barn cats who roamed the yard and barn at night looking for critters, but the snuffling didn't sound right, cats don't snuffle and ours would have probably tried to crawl into the sleeping bag with me for warmth, which I would have welcomed at that point. I looked across at my sister who was sound asleep not noticing a thing. I had had my head under the covers as I was cold and had discovered this helped me keep warm. Sleeping outdoors in summer, especially in western Washington, is a chilly affair.

Finally, I worked up the courage to see what had decided to repose at the foot of my "bed". I peered out. I could clearly make out something white in the darkness, sitting on the foot of my sleeping bag, sniffing around. It was a skunk! I didn't dare move. He was probably enjoying a little nighttime warmth there. I knew all about skunks. I knew how they smelled, I knew how they enjoyed the hen's eggs, not to mention, the hens, how they would take the lid off the garbage can and raid it for goodies. It only took one look. I just did the ostrich thing and pulled the covers back over my head. I could visualize having to throw away my brand new sleeping bag if this varmint decided to let go out of fright from encountering me underneath him. However, the visitor hung around the warmth for a while longer and then moseyed off to do whatever skunks do at night, eat chickens and such.

Since skunks could be a problem, my sis and I decided it would be best to move our sleeping arrangements to the barn loft which was half filled with hay. This became our preferred sleeping spot until the advent of the canvas wall tent. And besides, it smelled of wonderful hay. I made myself a cozy little nest of soft, loose hay surrounded by bales, like my own room, which afforded some privacy and warmth, but still allowed me to look out the large loft door at the sky where the stars were clearly visible. Pesky skunks could not climb the ladder to the loft, but the barn cats thought snuggling was pretty cool, or should I say warm.

Last night my husband and I slept under the stars for the umpteenth time in our lives. It is summer and this summer it's really summer. Living in western Washington, summer is an iffy thing. Usually three out of four Fourth of Julys it rains, which is better than having brush fires start from carelessly fired fireworks. This summer the days are dry and temperatures are in the seventies. Nights are in the low to mid fifties. It is clear. Since we live in the countryside, we can run around outside in the all together. (Maybe this is X rated) We can also sleep outside.

My husband and I started sleeping outside when we would take weekend trips to remote areas and sleep in the back of the station wagon. Traveling light was a necessity with two dogs and both of us working on Fridays with little time to pack efficiently. We needed room for a camp stove, not tents. And I had slept outside from a young age.

We could, and still can, hear all kinds of things at night. Coyotes howling at the moon in three part-harmonies for hours on end is one of the highlights. Deer walking within a couple of feet of our staked out territory. Mice ruffling though the dry leaves under the bed. Squirrels chipping at you in the morning. Racoons calling back and forth to one another, thinking about eating all those lovely chickens. In our farmyard the rooster starts crowing about 3:30 in the morning, or so my husband tells me. This morning it was the peahen at daybreak wondering where I was with her treat of corn. One of these mornings she'll probably discover where we are sleeping and give us her nasal, hollow-sounding honk right next to the bed. I am almost deaf, so cannot enjoy all the audio delights, it is all visual joys for me at this point in my life.

My sis and I slept on the ground, in the barn, in the woods, on the deck. We slept outside the night the first Sputnik crossed the sky and we could see its blinking light, or at least we were told that was what it was. It could have been a distant airplane, though you couldn't hear it.

The year of the Sputnik my bed was an aluminum chaise with woven plastic webbing on the patio.

At one time my sis and I decided it would be good to move to the barn loft, lots of hay for a bed and out of the rain. My sis had made a cozy spot for herself. When I awoke in the morning, she was gone. It was still pretty early, so I went back to sleep. Later when I went in the house for breakfast, my sis was real mad. It seems that her camping site was directly under the loft light fixture which had a swallows nest on top of it. The baby swallows were about to fledge and were standing around the edge of the nest making a lot of poop which fell directly on her head and face. Boy, was she mad and her new sleeping bag got its first washing. She found another place in the barn to sleep after checking for overhead objects before bedding down.

My trusty sleeping bag, purchased in 1954 was finally retired in 2015. It had a good life. Many years it was sleeping on the ground, sometimes on plastic and sometimes on grass. Plastic, we discovered, was too loud when you rolled over.

Sometimes it was camped in the back of the Volvo station wagon with the hatch open and our heads to the back so we could look out the rear hatch window at the sky. Some years it was in the hay in the hay loft of the barn and for a number of those iffy summers, in a walled army green tent.

Last night, Bob, my husband, and I settled down on our airbed mattress in the backyard, the more sophisticated arrangement we have now. It consists of a futon frame with an airbed mattress. We have sheets, pillows with cases and a big fluffy down quilt to keep warm and comfortable. Since it is a particularly dry year, we skipped the mosquito netting as they seem to have dried up. Some years they are voracious and as a result the netting is a necessity.

As I lay there, I thought about all the times we had done this. What is the attraction? Well, primarily looking up at the stars. At this point in my life it necessitates wearing my glasses, but without them I can still see misty spots in the sky and watch them pass overhead. Now when I wake up during the night, I can check their progress across the sky. At times we have tried to stay awake to see the Perseid star showers and have had some spectacular nights once they started. Usually two out of four years we get cloud cover for those days, so it is a treat to see them.

What else draws us to this? I thought..... the cool, refreshing breeze that literally caresses my face. Last night it was gentle, sweeping across my cheek and putting me to sleep like a gentle kiss. Sometimes the briskness of the air can be refreshing too with extra quilts piled on. Some years we have made it through late October before giving up for the season. Usually September is about the limit as the heavy dew or fog can make for very wet bedclothes. We have even tried to stay out during light rain, which is really nice on your face if it isn't getting everything too wet. The sun can dry out a light wetness during the day, but heavy rain requires throwing the handy piece of plastic over the whole thing and retreating to the bed in the house.

In 2014, when we had been sleeping outside for about a month, the night of August 11th, I made sure I had my glasses and went to bed to watch the Perseid meteor showers. I looked up, no stars. I looked again and since the sunset, and the sky had become dark, the clouds must have rolled in. Instead of the Perseid, we were treated to a wild and merry electrical display of lightning. At first, very loud and close. Our weather "Spark" (a modern phone app) warned us, the strike is within 2.3 miles, take cover. As the storm progressed it became heat lightning without the thunder but lots of light display.

A light drizzle started after I had been asleep for about an hour,. This was one of those intermittent, spitting drizzles. We decided to wait it out. It stopped a short while later and the bed driedout before we knew it. This was repeated about three times during the night, each time waking us up, but we enjoyed the refreshment it provided. It was a warm drizzle.

The next evening we were back outside, waiting for the clouds to clear. This was the last night that this year's meteor shower was to be visible. Clouds, Clouds, Clouds! We fell asleep. An hour later, the drizzle began again. We waited, trying to decide if it would be too wet, or if we can dry out between drizzles. No way. We covered the bed with plastic, headed in the house to sleep indoors. By the time we got up in the morning the drizzle had become a gully washer and .77 inches of rain had fallen. Good decision to retreat.

These days, it is pretty dark outside where we sleep, and Bob and I go out with a flashlight. A few seasons ago we pattered out to the bed parked in the orchard some distance from the house through our gardens to discover that there was an animal in the bed. The neighbor's cat thought this was a lovely place to sleep too.

Once when sleeping out in eastern Washington in the spring, we slept on the top of picnic tables because there were rattlesnakes around. The night was very cold. We didn't want any unwanted guests crawling in the bag with us for warmth. When we awoke in the morning the apple orchards nearby were covered in the most beautiful ice. To save the blossoms from frost, the orchardists turned on the irrigation sprinklers. This encases all the blossoms in ice, but saves them from damaging frost. It was almost as beautiful as the stars the night before.

Sleeping on the ground has its drawbacks. Well into my seventh decade, sleeping on a hard surface does not bode well for getting up off of said surface the next morning. Nor does it bode well for a happy day later either. Thus the more elaborate sleeping arrangements we use now. There is another drawback to sleeping on the ground which will wake you up with disgust. In our temperate climate zone we have a large population of slugs. I woke one night to something that felt like sucking on my neck. Washington State may have vampires in Forks, but those thirsty predators don't seem to populate the area around our house. I woke with a start and suddenly realized, IT WAS A SLUG, and it was crawling across my neck. This shelless mollusk leaves a diaphanous, gelatinous, slime trail. UGH! We don't like to even touch them around here and the goo is hard to remove from skin, requiring a scrub brush. This does not make for happy camping and happens more frequently when sleeping on plastic. Slugs like to hide under the dark damp material during the day and come out at night and crawl across your exposed skin. We wondered if the lariat trick worked for slugs, but it doesn't. The lariat trick, an old wives tale, was supposedly used by cowboys sleeping on the trail. If you opened your lariat to surround your bedroll, a rattlesnake would not go over it to snuggle with you.

Varmints can be a problem, earwigs, spiders, deer, coyotes, raccoons, cats, chickens. Four o'clock wake up calls from the rooster, midnight howls from coyotes or the neighbors malamute, cooing of the raccoons near enough you think they may want to bed down with you, pesky robins looking for worms in the flowerbed next to our bed or splashing in the birdbath in said flower bed, and more, can interrupt sleep. I have the advantage of not being able to hear most any longer unless I wear my hearing aids to bed. I like waking up to the birds, and I CAN hear some of them.

But.....if you have never slept outside without a tent, just lying on the ground or on an air mattress or in a hammock under the night sky, you are missing a wonderful treat. Try it just once and you will be hooked for life. It doesn't have to be in the back yard; it can be on a picnic table in a campground or on your apartment balcony. Privacy is nice, but not totally necessary. Do it with your kids sometime and start a lifetime tradition!

Fishing in Northern British Columbia

CHAPTER 17

Fishing

"The fishing was good; it was the catching that was bad." ~ *A. Best*

Moving to the country and living on a farm was very new for me, my sister and my mom. Of course, there were many wonders for us there including a new school, a big garden, and eventually a horse, chickens, pigs, and cows. It was strange to have so much space around us.

Down at the bottom of the pasture and over a couple of fences was Bear Creek. We were about a quarter mile from its confluence with the Sammamish River. I always pictured creeks as small waterways populated with lots of frogs and tadpoles. This creek had areas that were thigh deep, not deep enough to swim, but good wading and cooling in the summer. You could sit in the water and it would come up to your chest. In places it was twenty feet wide.

Back then mothers didn't worry if they didn't see their kids for six or seven hours at a time. They were thankful to be rid of the kids for a few hours of peace. Sis and I would pack a lunch and take off, sometimes on a horse and sometimes walking. Some days with a fishing pole in hand. The horse couldn't come fishing because of the fences, though she would have loved to stand in the creek and cool her heels.

I learned that I loved to fish. Of course, I always had to take my little sister with me on these forays. The problem was that she tended to stomp around in the water when I was trying to fish. Fish don't much enjoy someone stomping around, so they moved onto less turbulent regions. I was glad for a little freedom, if not quiet with my sister making such splashes and fuss. She would be bored and wanted to go home. OK. Go home. Of course, she wouldn't leave without me as she was probably only five or six. She would look for stuff. Stuff included fresh water eels, freshwater clams, pretty rocks, gold (which was fool's gold), and anything else of interest. If it was hot, we both would just sit in the water which wasn't very deep.

I fished and fished and fished. Over the four or five years we lived there, I caught one fish. It was a small rainbow trout. I have to confirm that it was SMALL. I probably should have thrown it back, but that concept had not been delivered to me when I was told the rules about fishing. No deep water, no fast water, don't drink the water, and don't eat your sandwich if it has fallen in the water. Nothing about taking a trout that probably didn't equal seven inches.

I brought my trophy home. I was so proud of this fish. By this time I had probably been fishing for several years. I had had only a few bites, but I was not daunted by the lack of response of the part of the fishes. Well, when I took the fish home, since it was too small for dinner, my mom suggested that we freeze it until I got another. How likely was that? I had already been fishing a couple of years to catch this one. Well, the answer was never.

We moved a couple of times and the freezer came with us. When I was in high school, I was assigned the project of defrosting the freezer. This is probably six or eight years after having caught the fish. There it was in the freezer, light as a feather. Still shining in all its rainbow glory, but not something you would want to cook unless you were starving. I tossed him out. I think I probably could have nailed him to the wall as a trophy and he probably wouldn't have even smelled he was so desiccated by freezer burn. So much for a momentous family moment.

In later years when I was on my own, I had little money and practically scavenged what I ate. I would get giant packages of chicken backs for five cents a pound and bake or stew them for what little meat they offered. I purchased five cent a pound beef kidneys and ate them. I also fished.

Fishing was a Saturday project. My parents had moved to the Eddie Bauer homestead while I was away at college. This homestead included a large pond stocked with cutthroat trout. Every Saturday morning, I would go out and sit by the pond with my book and fish. When I had captured enough for two meals for the week, I would stop. I would have two dinners of wonderful fresh trout. The rest of the week was kidneys and chicken backs. I know at least fifteen ways to fix cutthroat trout, chicken scraps and kidneys.

Not so many years ago, a neighbor invited us to go salmon fishing. I think that he just invited my husband, Bob, but I invited myself as well. Off to Saratoga Passage to a "hot spot" that only he knew and we commenced to fish. We trolled some (dragged a baited line behind a slow moving boat). We caught dogfish, a form of shark that most either kill or throw back. They make pretty good fertilizer too. I was steadily catching Dover sole at the turn around point for the boat as it was shallower there. The neighbor and my husband didn't have much success with catching the salmon, but by the time they gave up I had five sole. I was never invited to go fishing with them again. The sole were delicious!

My husband's family lived in Eastern Montana. They had a summer cabin at Fort Peck Lake. A couple of times we went out in a boat with my father-in-law, but one day he and his dad were busy, so I took the pole down the road a ways and cast into the water. I caught five fairly large fish. I was pretty excited and since it was warm and I didn't have a way to keep them cool, I decided that I should probably head back. They saw me coming and started laughing. I didn't understand. "Why did you bring those carp home?! Nobody eats those!" I didn't know they were junk fish, but we kept them and gave them to my father-in-law's neighbor who was from Russia and loved them. At least someone appreciated my fishing skills. She gave me six antique canning jars in trade.

When we lived in China, we ate LI (carp) may times and it was delicious. It is steamed and served with ginger and scallions with a sauce that has soy. My students would order this for special occasions. Carp is bony, but eating it with chopsticks peeled the flesh easily from the bones.

Now I am on the downhill side of life. We go camping on occasion and I am thinking of becoming a worm dangler with a book again. When we are camping, why not put a hook in the water and read a good book? I think that I may become a fisherwoman again.

Modern Day Foraging on Ebey's Prairie—Painting by D. Matzen

CHAPTER 18

Foraging in the Burbs

"A man who chases two rabbits catches none."--Roman proverb

Growing up, we had apple trees, but we wrapped the apples in paper and stored them through the winter to eat and bake. I still do this from the trees on our property. They are "keepers" and will taste good and crispy until about May. Mostly the horse ate what she could reach in the tree. Sometimes we would stand on her back and reach more for her. She was always game to stand still under the tree when it was filled with apples.

When I was growing up and living in Redmond we had a group of folks who foraged for a different product. Lake Sammamish flooded most winters and the Sammamish River hadn't been damaged by the Bureau of Reclamation yet. When they straightened the river, the lake no longer flooded. The north end of the lake where the outflow became the Sammamish River there was a marshy area like a bayou. This was the home to thousands of bullfrogs. Yum. Foragers had shallow draft boats that would appear there at night with men who stood in the boats with lights to gaff the frogs. These were sold for the legs. I have to admit I am particularly fond of this dish.

We had a pond on the Eddie Bauer farm where I lived, the one when I was in college. My uncle came to visit and he liked the frog's legs as much as we did. His trick to catch them was to use a fishing pole with a small piece of red flannel tied to the hook. The bullfrogs would go for it every time.

I guess I should qualify this whole process with the information that bullfrogs are an invasive species in our area, just like those vicious blackberries. They destroy the habitat for the native frogs which are rapidly losing ground in modern times. So don't be feeling too sorry for those bullfrogs.

Well friends of ours from school wanted to go frog hunting and came to the farm to try it. We used the nighttime method rather than my uncle's daytime method. With flashlight in hand we waded on the fringes of the pond and shone the light on a frog. Our partner would grab the frog which was temporarily blinded by the light. Just like catching chickens in the henhouse at night. It was warm out as it was summer. I had on shorts and was wandering in the shallows when I walked straight into the electric fence. It got me across both thighs with a loud zap. I screamed and it was the end of frog hunting for the night as they all headed to deeper water. I had a burn across both legs. Luckily electric fences are required to pulse so you can let go and not be electrocuted. I still love frog legs, but I buy them at the Chinese grocery now. We don't have bullfrogs that I know on Whidbey.

When I moved to Whidbey Island the beginning of the 1970s, it was a quiet sleepy little farm community. Folks raised sheep and cows, pigs, and chickens. Brush picking was a big industry. There were more retired folks and summer folks than students in the school district. We had one campus in Langley, the only incorporated town on the south end of the island.

I met people who had moved here from Norway, Sweden, Ireland in the '20s, '30s, and '40s. Back when the steamboat was the only regular way to get here if you didn't own your own boat. Many locals had a side occupation as woodcutters, cutting lengths of wood from the local forests to fuel the steamboat . Glendale, which is about a mile from my house, was a stop for the steamboat where it took on small logs there to fuel the boilers. There still stands a building which was a hotel for travelers before they traveled inland up a narrow canyon filled with a small creek and lots of forest.

In more recent times, this road has seen several washouts from the creek and mudslides are frequent in this cut in the land. Trees tumble across the road as they slide down the steep hillsides. It is a dank, dark region, reminiscent of "Sleepy Hollow."

A few years ago a lake about three or so miles from this area had its dam break, a dam which had been created by a beaver. Beaver farming was an industry here in the early 1900's and I have a friend who lives on a former beaver farm. Well, sometime in the distant past some of these beautiful critters got loose in the wild, became an invasive species, and one had build a dam on the creek that goes to Glendale. A beautiful ten acre pond was the result. The man who owned the land with the pond was happy to have the pond. But...a year or two ago, someone hit the beaver while he was crossing the road a ways away from his dam. The dam fell into disrepair and eventually broke. Ten acres of water went roaring down the canyon. Debris forced ahead of the water piled up against a culvert in the road and the pressure of the water took the debris and the road with it. The county finally decided that they would vacate the road and now it is a reminder of what water can do to a county road.

The little settlement of Glendale with its twenty or so houses was flooded, again. The old hotel had a couple of feet of mud in the first floor. A lot of work was required to make these houses habitable. The locals still talk about the time the beaver died and the road was washed out and the Glendale flood. Even though Glendale had been flooded more than once, we always know which flood they are mentioning.

My husband and I used to forage apples to make cider every October. Everyone around here did that. Many seedling trees grow on the county right-of-way roads. My Irish friends from Cork had a press at their home in Brighton Beach near Clinton, and we would all gather at their house with our barrels of washed apples and press all day. Usually the weather was very cold and crisp with a weak sun lighting the day of the pressing. One gallon jug would have a little rum (or a lot) added to it to keep those of us who were getting wet during the process, warm. Often times that jug would get confused with the others and we would have to make up another. Hopefully, the kids didn't get it with their Cheerios in the morning. It was always a big deal and a great party we all looked forward to. We all brought something on which to snack and there was hot food and coffee to keep us warm as well as a bonfire on the beach. My Irish friends lived on the beach so the kids would play on the shoreline in the driftwood all day.

We would take home ten or fifteen gallons of cider, having shared some with those who helped but didn't have access to apples. I would can the cider and we would have it to drink all winter. Some folks made hard cider and we usually saved out a gallon to drink when it started to get bubbly.

We became friends with one lady who gave us apples. She had arrived from Norway about 1914 and her childhood home still stands on Highway 525 near the Clinton Ferry. Winter Banana was one variety she had. She lived in Clinton until she married and then moved to Deer Lagoon to a big farm with her husband. They planted many apple trees which she didn't prune or pick anymore because of her age and lack of agility. She would let us come and pick the apples if we would bring her a little cider, something we were happy to do. She would tell us tales about her young life and the steamboat that brought goods and folks to the island. Her dad had worked as a woodcutter.

The modern version of this whole scene in the suburbs today is as follows: Once a year in the fall, the local citified farm and garden store here on the island has a cider pressing day. You can bring your own apples and have them pressed or you can buy them at the grocery or farmers market to press. The city folks make a quart or two of cider and take it home. Many of the old trees are still around the island, but most of the new folks won't let you pick them because they are afraid of liability. Don't want you falling off a ladder under their trees. They usually just let the apples rot on the ground. The deer do get some of them. Sad, it is a waste of food and the cider was wonderful heated on a cold winter's evening.

Brush picking was another early occupation on the island besides woodcutting. When I moved here, it was still a big business. Brush picking was the pruning and cutting of the undergrowth of the forests of the island. We have a lot of evergreen huckleberry, salal, Oregon grape, ferns, and few other kinds of flora that were the mainstay of the florists in the city for the greenery in bouquets they sold in town. The brush pickers drove trucks with high, extended racks on the back to be filled with the leafy cuttings from the woods.

When we used to go walking in the woods, you would sometimes find a fire circle of rocks and know that the brush pickers had made camp there to fill their trucks. They would build a fire to eat a midday meal since it is wet work and they would need warming. They used a strange tool that attached to their index finger and thumb that allowed them to use a pinching motion to scissor off a branch from the bushes. Must have had really strong hands. The brush picking was beneficial to the plants as they produced more berries in the fall. Brush pickers never took too much as this would cut into their future business. They were good caretakers of the land. They picked all over the island and you would occasionally see signs “no brush picking” around here. Most folks didn’t mind as they didn’t leave trash or broken branches, just the little fire rings where they had heated their mid-day meal.

Now we forage for blackberries (see chapter 18) and for blue huckleberries. The blue huckleberry grows all around our house. They are a real treat, but very small and tedious to pick. We didn’t have them in the area where I grew up, but they are abundant here. I will pick a cupful for muffins, but seldom have the energy to manage enough for pie. I have made jam from them and with a little orange zest added, they taste very similar to black currant. Unfortunately, they are so small, that I seldom make the effort. The robins gorge on them when they migrate though in the fall and the bushes around the house look like bears are attacking them, they sway so much outside our windows. Luckily we don’t have bears as these are a favorite food of theirs.

Other berries that are edible and make decent jelly are salal and Oregon grape. Both have very tough skins, but may be used in combination with blackberries, wild strawberries etc. for bumble berry jam. Salal is very tart and a nice addition crushed in salad dressing. As far as munching on these two berries, you would have to be pretty hungry. Flowering red currant is best left for the birds.

Brush pickers use to have a sideline business and one in which I liked to participate, mushrooming. Whidbey has many types of edible mushrooms. I have gathered only the chanterelles and the morels. The morels I collected were a side benefit of the growth of the island into the burbs. The local soil distributor apparently had morel mycelium mixed in with his bark which he distributed to all those city folks that needed a manicured yard. The morels came up in all of them. I looked in every flower bed around my travels. I found them at the place that cut my hair. I asked if they wanted them and they just said ugh and turned up their noses. I picked them for dinner. I would have loved to get the list of deliveries from this company as I could have had lots for several weeks, their window of availability. At the Pike Place Market in Seattle, the only place I have seen them for sale, they were over $30 per pound. I was in heaven. Their rich smoky flavor is wonderful with veal or chicken in a cream sauce on homemade pasta.

The chanterelles are more common. Their habitat is under the salal in pine forests. This is the same area where the brush pickers were working. I bet they even sautéed some to go with their lunches. It is wet work looking for chanterelles. The salal is hip to chest height. It is a large, glossy leafed plant that holds water when it rains. Chanterelles appear after the first rains of fall. Traipsing through chest high wet foliage can be cold work, but under the salal is the lovely golden yellow-orange chanterelle. I have picked bucketsful, but they do not freeze well and mold if you try to keep them long. Some have tried drying them, but I haven't.

I worked for about twelve years teaching at the local community college which was located in a strip mall on the highway. The strip mall backed onto a quite dense forest. One of my older (in his 80's) students got to class early one day and decided to take a walk in the woods before class. He always wore a fedora. He showed up in class with a present for me. Nestled in his fedora was a giant mound of the largest chanterelles I had ever seen. He said, “I went for a little walk and found these for you.” There must have been two pounds. He had collected them in ten minutes. Did he get a good grade for the day?

When this student passed away recently, I went to his memorial service and was asked to speak a little about him. I related that story of his gift to me and what a generous person he had always been. I miss him. He taught me a lot.

We also have shaggy manes (very fragile) and chicken-of-the-woods, which I have not tried. I have friends who say these are their favorites. Occasionally I hear of lion’s manes too which are supposed to be a real delicacy. I have seen them, but not eaten them. I tried “seeding” oyster mushroom mycelium in alder stumps on my land, but without luck.

Being a wet wooded island, we have lots of ferns. I have tried foraging for ferns and I have read as much as I could find about cooking the fiddleheads, but have never felt comfortable about eating them. When they were steaming, the strong smell of bitter almonds filled the whole house. I have read you must change the water several times to make them edible. Edible, the strong smell of bitter almonds seems too much like cyanide for my liking and I understand that there are varieties which contain this. Forget fiddleheads until I find someone who knows more about this delight?

The wild cherries and plums in our area are left for the birds. They are very small with large full sized pits and little flesh which is terribly bitter.

The red huckleberry grows around the house as well. The birds like it. I eat them when I am working outside as they are tart, bright red-orange little spheres which easily will quench your thirst. They are good to pick as you walk on a hike too. I made jam from them and entered it in the county fair about thirty years ago and the judge asked why I bothered as the old-timers didn’t bother with them.

A distillery in Portland, Oregon recently made a eau-de-vie from Douglas fir bough tips. We purchased a small bottle, but it tastes like drinking freshly cut lumber. Not my taste at all. Friends have suggested that the new fir tips in the spring taste good too, but I tried them and unless I was starving, probably wouldn't eat very many. One short-lived bottled water company touted their product was collected from the fir tips as the rainwater dripped from them. Sounds like an expensive process. Never tried it. I have licked the raindrops from the tips of the branches when hiking in the woods, probably not a very sanitary thing to do with bird poop in trees.

We have a plant in the woods here called Indian potato, but it is so small it is not worth collecting. The camas lily on Ebey's Prairie was a food staple for the Northwest Indians who spent summers collecting it and clams here on the island. It is protected now so we cannot dig it. Only the blue flowering variety is edible.

Clams, well that is another foraging bonanza. We have a number of beaches which are suitable nearby. Clams here like gravel which makes for hard digging. When we first came here, there were no licenses required, and no limits, though we would limit ourselves for their preservation. Clamming today is a much more regulated process. First, there must be a low tide. Very low. Gravel that is about the size of a dime to a quarter is the nesting place of the butter clam, my favorite. One of the problems today is the growth of the island has caused problems with pollution and some beaches are closed due to leaking sewage from nearby household drainfields. We also have issues with red tide, an algae that turns the ocean bright red and cause the shellfish to be toxic if eaten. You need a permit and you are restricted to the number of clams you may take. If you crush one accidently, you can no longer give it to the gulls, it must be counted in your limit. You MUST, and this is important, refill the hole you have dug. You will get a ticket if you don't.

If you don't fill in the hole, the young clams will be washed out of the hole by the incoming tide and die.

Yes, you can get tickets, too many clams, not filling in holes, not having the proper endorsement on your fishing license. How do you get a ticket? The Fish and Wildlife department of the State of Washington patrols beaches to be sure the regulations are followed. Your endorsement must hang on the outside of your clothing in plain sight for the officer to see with binoculars from his vehicle or from a great distance down the beach or from his boat. It is a good thing too because many new folks think this clam digging is a free-for-all and don't even bother to read the rules. If we want to have these for the future, we need to be good stewards today.

Bob and I prefer mussels which live on the rocks and do not require digging and filling of holes. They are tastier too and less apt to crack your teeth biting on the occasional small stone within clams. The same pollution problems and licensing apply, but they are much easier to "stalk." We can also buy them here as there are large commercial businesses raising them in our waters. Yum. They also certify that they have not been affected by red tide and therefore not poisonous. We prepare these with tomatoes, onions, garlic and white wine and eat them with toasty Italian bread that I make. There is a restaurant up island that serves them twelve different ways. Great place to eat.

Fishing is another foraging method. During a certain time of year, you can fish for salmon right from the beach. You can even catch whoppers. People limit out daily. My brother-in-law bought a boat in his retirement and we benefit from the surplus fish he catches, salmon, cod, and my favorite, crab. He and my sis can take five a day apiece and they frequently share, so we have a nice diet of crab in the summer months. Cracked crab for the first few meals of the season and then on to crab cakes with garlic aioli and crab melts. Crab doesn't freeze too well as it can get stringy, but crab cakes do ok if you don't leave them in the freezer too long. So this foraged item needs to be eaten right away and cannot be put away for other seasons. Gorge while it is available.

We have another invasive species on the beaches, the little green crab. It is about the size of a quarter and when you turn over large rocks, there are a bunch of the pesky little things. I keep threatening to try deep fat frying them in the shell until it is crispy and eating them whole dipped in red pepper rouille or garlic aioli sauce. We have eaten winkles and the dog winkle here is edible though we haven't tried it yet. Sea cucumber is delicious but more tedious to prepare. Tastes like chicken! No it doesn't taste like chicken. It tastes like abalone which is endangered in many parts of the world including a small variety which is here.

We used to have pheasants here, but no longer. Too bad, because I always loved pheasant, even though you must take care when preparing them as they can be tough and dry. I remember when we moved to our first farm we had a very large picture window in the living room. One day there was a terrible thump and when we went to see what it was a pheasant had hit the window. He was lying in the flower bed under the window. My mom rushed out, broke its neck and we had it for dinner. My dad use to bring them home when he went to eastern Washington hunting. But they are rare these days here and we never see them on our end of the island.

Crawdads are my next pursuit. The local lake has them and I would like to catch a mess. I have to get a crawdad trap as the crab traps have holes which are too big. Maybe that will be my next challenge. Several lakes near our home here have them. It is best if the lake is pretty cold. The largest lake here is too warm for them to be tasty.

We used to purchase a lamb every year from friends who raised them for us until butcher time. We would have wonderful lamb to eat all winter. Now farms are smaller and we have a lot of city folks who commute across the water to work. The cost of living has increased considerably. A short while back, I called a friend who raises sheep for milk to make cheese she sells at the farmers market and to restaurants in Seattle. She had lamb for sale and I asked about ground lamb. Unfortunately, it was $12.99 a pound. We cannot afford meat that expensive, not steak and certainly not ground lamb. Maybe we should think about raising one ourselves. I checked on wiener pigs last spring. We sold ours when I was a kid for $5. It takes a lot of scraps and feed to make a butcher weight hog. The wiener pigs were $100 each making the cost of a chop on a finished animal about $12 per pound. Just not worth the trouble or the expense. I guess there are folks who pay that much for meat, and apparently they will pay $25 a pound for cheese as well.

We had a weed in our garden that we liked to eat. It was Shepherd's Purse. It tastes similar to arugula. I tended to overgraze and now it no longer comes up in the garden. I was surprised to hear from my Chinese friend that this is something they really like in China. She stir fries it. When she was going to school in Reno, she spied it in a city park and she and a friend picked a large basket of it several times. Urban foraging. Hope she washed it well.

We had friends who made wine from all sorts of things including one from rhubarb and another from pea vines. The rhubarb is good, but the pea vine did not suit my tastes. Parsnips are one veggie I do not eat. I have even tried parsnip wine in hopes this horrible vegetable would have some redeeming quality. It didn't. Carrot wine, parsley wine. I guess that folks will try to turn almost anything with a little sugar into alcohol. Doesn't mean it will taste good.

The chickens are probably the best foragers here on the farm. They will eat almost anything except slugs, which we have in abundance. Ducks will eat slugs, but ducks are messy and always wanted to stand on the porch. Chickens eat all the bugs they can find. They do eat the earthworms too, but can't dig too deep so most of the worms are safe. They are good at cleaning the weeds seeds from the garden and eating the bugs from there too. I give them the weeds from the flower beds and they think these are a special treat. In return, I dig out the hen yard and get wonderful hummusy soil for the flower beds and garden. It is dark and rich and the vegetables and flowers love it. Doesn't cost me much either.

Nettles are a common spring vegetable and not unique to this area. I have a Cajun recipe for Lenten Gumbo which calls for nettles, so they are pretty universal. Ours are stinging nettles and pretty nasty if not handled correctly. Heavy gloves are required when harvesting. Most folks here who use them make tea as the nettle is high in iron and vitamin C. Beware of breathing the steam when cooking as the stinging portion vaporizes with the steam and you can get a very nasty rash. We tend to pull them and put them in the compost as consuming them is not a family favorite in our household.

Filberts (hazelnuts) grow wild here and there are some groves which were commercial, but no longer actively harvested. They are great if you can manage to beat the Stellar's jay to them. Jays are particularly fond of them and hide them in holes and cavities of trees for later consumption. I use to have a small grove of them on a piece of property I owned in my early adulthood and it was always a challenge to harvest some before the jays managed to steal them all. In Oregon they are now raising truffles on filbert roots. I love toasted filberts with a glass of port in the evening in the winter. Such a treat.

Whidbey has truffles as well and there is an annual class in the fall provided by a person who teaches dogs to search for them. I have found only one while digging around the gardens on our property. It has only been the last few years that anyone knew they grew here. I would think it would take quite a while to train a dog to be a truffle hunter. I should live so long.

We don’t go after the squirrels or the cottontails, but I certainly have threatened them many a time and I may yet decide to make squirrel gumbo. Raccoons are supposed to taste like pork and I would love to do away with those varmints who are so destructive to my chickens and the fish in my ponds. There are some here who hunt the deer, but we haven’t gotten into something that large. I love the taste of venison, but it would be a project bigger than I feel I could handle. I do enjoy being given a piece or two occaisionally. Duck hunting is now forbidden, and Canada geese are tough critters.

I am sure there is more to forage here, but these are just some of the things we have either eaten or considered eating. You would never starve here, though you might not want to try to survive by foraging if you had better choices.

I grew up in a frugal family who never let anything go to waste. I guess I’m no different.

Great Blackberry Territory in Old Farmsteads—Painting by D. Matzen

CHAPTER 19

In Pursuit of the Wild Blackberry.

(I originally wrote this chapter for my Advanced English Writing students in Beijing Foreign Studies University as an example of descriptive writing.)

Blackberries are an abundant and wonderful fruit that is free for the taking in the Maritime Northwest. You could pick truckloads if you wanted. I could pick and sell them to the local pie shop, but I don't. Some years are really good and some years it rains and they all mildew making them inedible.

This is not the tiny little seedless thing (Rubusursinus) that grows along the ground and over your favorite, recently transplanted annuals, but the large luscious briar patch type (Himalayan--Rubusarmeniacus) or the Evergreen(which is deciduous, not evergreen as its name would lead us to believe--**Rubuslaciniatus).All are related to roses. Roses have thorns and so do blackberries.**

Both the Himalaya and Evergreen varieties are invasive species in our country. Luscious though they may be, they are, indeed, invasive and considered a noxious weed in areas of Washington State,. They grow everywhere, and if you wait long enough to do something about them, they can totally devour your house, car, and your children, should they stand still long enough. They are dangerous and treacherous to navigate, sending out eight to ten foot tendrils covered with vicious thorns worse than those on roses. They are what the name briar patch is all about, creating a dense, nest-like mound that is a perfect hiding place for birds, rabbits, mice and more. When the coyote calls, the varmints head for the briar patch. This is the reason Br'er Rabbit asked not to be thrown there, because it was actually his best hiding place.

Many things have been discovered in blackberry patches when it has become time to obliterate one. The brush munchers that are so popular for clearing brush these days find all sorts of metal things enshrouded in blackberries patches; old trucks, tires and wheels, anything someone forgot or wanted to hide. If you could manage to hollow out a large enough area inside they would make a great secret place, totally protected from intruders.

Though these beasties are invasive, they are amongst some of the most wonderful free bounty we enjoy where I live. I can remember a friend and I--I was about 10 at the time and new to the countryside-- were out running around the neighborhood and I saw these berries. She said try one, they won't hurt you. I loved it. We looked around for some cleaned, used tin cans and picked and picked and picked. I took home about a gallon to my mom. All she could say was "They have too many seeds." She liked the miniscule ones (Rubusursinus)that are virtually seedless, and take 100 years to pick a tin can full.

Well, I did convince her to make a cobbler which I thought was wonderful. The aromatics of the berry will take your breath away. The house was filled with the musky, dark, pungent sweetness of the bubbling cobbler. They ARE juicy and large and full of seeds. Seeds are a good source of fiber unless you suffer from diverticulitis, in which case, your doctor would advise against them.

My sister and I were the self-appointed berry pickers, and though there was little enthusiasm from my mom, she would make a cobbler for us if we did the picking. We would head out to the local berry picking grounds and pick to our hearts content, eating all the while. Growing up in Redmond, Washington, summers were hot when I was a kid. Mid to late August, the air is fragrant with the sticky, fruity smell of blackberries. It is one of the very fond memories of summertime, still is, though the summers don't seem as hot and the scent seems less strong. Maybe one of the reasons is I live on an island now and the seacoast may cause more breeze in the summer and not the suffocating, oppressive heat of my childhood.

Many times my sister and I were so enthused about the picking we were not watching where we were going. On one occasion, my sister looked up and said "Help. I'm surrounded by stinging nettles", something that frequently grows interspersed with the berries, another acid soil loving menace. She could not spy the way she had entered the maze. "Help me get out." I couldn't find the way either, but I could see her. Berry picking season is usually hot and she was wearing a sleeveless shirt for the occasion. Not the best idea, but if you are careful you won't get raked by the vicious berries and your sleeves won't get torn on the tenacious thorns.

Finally, I told her I just couldn't see any way out, "Just turn your head to avoid the stings on the face and plow through." She didn't want to lose any precious berries, so she held her two buckets up over her head and plowed through. Consequently, she had stinging nettle blisters in her armpits, one of the most sensitive and worst spots to be stung. She spent the next several days plastered with calamine lotion. Boy, was the cobbler good.

When I moved to the city there was a big blackberry patch on a vacant lot just down the street, vacant lots making ideal environments for blackberries. Besides invading any vacant, deserted location, they cover up the detritus left there from previous occupants. I made blackberry champagne. Ah, what a wonderful delight and one I should pursue now. We have an abundance here in the countryside near the house and we make thick, gooey pies and dark, musky jelly (without the seeds, but with the pulp) every year canning enough jelly to eat until the next season arrives. We also eat a ton of them right off the bushes when out walking the dog. They are great thirst quenchers when hiking too, and abundant on almost all trails. The coyotes eat all the lower ones up as high as they can reach and leave very seedy piles of poop in the street to bear witness. (in wild plum season, there are piles of plum seeds)

My nephew came to visit from Montana one year when blackberries were in season and fell in love with them. Fell in more ways than one. When he picked all the berries that he could reach from the roadside across the street from our driveway, he came back to the house and asked for a ladder. My husband let him take the orchard ladder out to the street. Needless to say the best, ripest, and biggest berries were just out of reach, even from the ladder. The wooden orchard ladder has three legs which is perfect for uneven ground, but before he knew it, he had fallen into the briar patch. He was in about six feet and totally entrapped by the vicious, but luscious berries. His clothes were completely entangled. He was like a fly in a spider's web and could not move or help himself out. We heard his calls and finally came to the rescue with a large plank. He practically had to disrobe to get out and almost required stitches to repair his lacerations, but he still said it was worth it just to have the pie.

My brother-in-law, also from Montana where they do not have these treats, went out to pick one afternoon when he arrived before I got home from work. He knew that I always had pie crusts made up in the freezer and started a pie from his bounty. There were so many berries they wouldn't fit into a pie tin, so he used my 10" cast iron frying pan to make the double crust pie. It was beautiful when it came out of the oven. Dark, very large, filled with a steaming, bubbling filling that was both aromatic and had a dark mystery.

I can tell you now, don't do this. Don't cook blackberries in cast iron. We ate the pie and it was delicious. As wonderful as you can possibly image, however,...... when we looked at each other, our mouths were BLACK. Black beyond belief. Our lips, and tongues and probably stomachs were black. We still looked like we had some form of plague in the morning. If you do bake it in cast iron, plan on staying home for several days or you will scare anyone you meet.

A friend of mine decided to retire in the warmer climes of southern California. I heard from her recently and she mentioned that the blackberry doesn't grow near her. I suppose there are regions there where they grow, but not near her. She said that it was three years before she could bring herself to actually purchase blackberries in the store. Why would you pay for them? I guess she was finally desperate enough and decided she would pay the price. Her comment: they were hard and sour and nothing like the wonderful free ones we have here.

Even though they are pests, the invasive species of Himalayan and Evergreen blackberries are a treat worth the effort. August is the time, though in June and July, the flowers make a great source of honey in our area. If you are visiting, I suggest that it is worth trying them, but be sure not to get trapped as it could require a trip to the hospital.

International Kite Festival Winning Poster Art—w/c by D. Matzen

CHAPTER 20

FAIR TIME (earlier)

"There is something that feels so all-American about a county fair."--Anonymous

It is July and it is fair time. I was always a pretty active participant in the fair, bringing goods and winning ribbons was lots of fun. That was forty years ago. The fair has changed considerably in more recent times.

It is still the fair, but it is no longer run by the county and therefore not a "county" fair. It is the Whidbey Island Fair run now by the Island County Port Commission.

During the transition from one system to another some important things were neglected, the major one being the booking of the carnival folks. We always had the fair around the middle of August when things were hot and dusty, when the gardens were producing lots of veggies and fruits. Now the fair is the middle of July, much too early for an agricultural event.

What happened? When the port realized that they hadn't booked the carnival, it wasn't available and there weren't any others available for the usual time frame, mid August. What to do? Well you need a carnival for the fair in order to attract lots of folks and the only one available was available way too early for an agricultural event. They booked it and moved the fair up a month.

What were the repercussions of this sad move? The carnival activities look ok, though this concessionaire is smaller and doesn't have the usual Ferris wheel or roller coaster or hammer. The rides aren't as exciting.

The biggest repercussion is the agriculture events. How many folks in Western Washington (night temps in the 50s) have corn ready to show at the fair in July? Only strawberries have ripened in time. You should see the examples of garlic, beans, and squash. Piddily. Most of the produce is just coming on and showing juvenile veggies is not what the fair is about. There were flowers, but they were early summer ones not late summer, a completely different collection than what we used to see. Folks can't get inspired to show their wares if they are still immature.

Cattle, pigs, sheep are still somewhat under their usual August weights. The livestock auctions bring in smaller dollar amounts. Horses are ready any time as are the chickens, rabbits, dogs, cats, and such.

When I first moved to the island and lived in a Clinton beach community, the local kids and I would go on walkabout and collect shells, sea glass, seed pods, driftwood, and rocks and work on project gluing these to plywood or larger driftwood to enter the kid's crafts. It was fun and they treasured the ribbons given to them for their labors. Nowadays the kids are on computers or cell phones and don't collect detritus from the beach to make beach collages. Too bad because the exhibit was painfully lacking in interesting material.

Photography seemed to be popular with hundreds of participants, but most were just snapshots from cellphones without much concentration on creating a piece of art. The fine arts exhibition was beautiful with a variety of participants, but smaller than in past years.

The usual commercial exhibits didn't show because the attendance wasn't high enough—no vegamatic salesman.

We usually go on the first day of the fair in order to see the flowers and vegetables and baked goods at their best, before the wilt and mold set in. Baking was poorly attended, but there were a goodly number of flowers. Vegetables were, and have been for all the years the fair has been in July, small, and severely lacking. It used to be my favorite department and I would always participate. Unfortunately, this year, the weather has not cooperated especially, with temps in the 50s at night and 60s during the day and rain to damage much of the goods.

My painting students produced an educational project that garnered a blue ribbon. I won two blues and a red. Many of my students achieved the blue ribbon and some the best of category. I am proud of them. The judge was fair and did write critiques for them to read about their work. It is good to compete as you put your best foot forward and work on painting harder. The rewards reinforce their attempts. Not everyone goes home happy, but most are happy. I will crack the whip next year to get them to compete again.

All in all, I enjoyed my work time at the fair (4 hours) as I got to see old friends, some of whom I hadn't seen in years, many of whom I have known as long as I have lived here (almost fifty years) and one who I have known since high school. It becomes a reunion time. Some of the kids from the beach collage days are parents and grandparents now. It is good to see their development. Some of the folks ask questions and one family had only lived here a week. They were really enthusiastic about the country fair never having been to a small, old fashioned one.

I had my Fisher Flour Mill scone which I have had at the fair as long as I have lived here. When I was a little kid we went to the Puyallup Fair, which is officially the Western Washington State Fair and had a scone at the Fisher booth. My sister and I would collect coupons off the flour sacks all year so we could each have a free scone with strawberry jam using the coupons. I am told the line is very long now, though I haven't been to that fair in years, too commercial. We don't get free scones any more, however.

Without a doubt I enjoyed myself and maybe I should work to make it a better event. We need to keep these small fairs going, they are dying out in America and they are what the county or country fair is really about. You should seek them out and visit. They are truly a part of the vanishing rural America.

More recent:

I have just completed about ten days helping with the Fine Arts exhibit at the county fair. Wow, was that intensive. It was a lot of work in a freezing WPA building (Roosevelt's New Deal) made from logs. It was a wind tunnel and each day I returned home with a wind burned face and freezing cold. It is July and this is supposed to be summer?

Earlier in the year I was asked if I would be willing to apprentice to become the superintendent of the Adult Fine Arts area of the county fair. Since I had recently lost my teaching job due to Covid, I thought this might be a good thing to do; after all, it is only a couple of weeks in July, a month we normally do not go camping.

As a participant in the show for many years (40 plus) I knew fairly well what the job entailed. Firstly, we needed to prepare the premium book for our department with the "rules and regulations" of competition. We needed to decide what information should be on the tickets attached to the paintings for the show—this is an online item to be completed by the artist. Then for a full day the intake of works from the artists (ten hours). Next the show needed to be hung in order for the judge to judge the paintings in situ. The fair uses the Danish rating system where each piece is judged by its own merits. When judging is completed, the tags are printed from the computer and the ribbons are attached to each piece. Every entry gets a ribbon of some type—blue, red, or white. A few receive special recognition for being best of oil, watercolor, acrylic, drawing, etc. We received one hundred and forty entries. Finally the show was ready, after four or five days of preparation, we were ready for four days of fair activities..

Now the fun part begins. This year's fair had a record attendance with approximately 22,000 folks attending. We didn't have all of these coming through our exhibit, but we did have lots. This is a small county country fair. It still is old –fashioned and very reminiscent of the country fairs from the '40s and '50s though we no longer have the greased pig race or calf roping or the barnyard scramble, though there is baking, sewing, quilt show, flowers, vegetables and fruits, sheep, cows, rabbits, dogs, guinea pigs, goats, pigs, horses and much more.

There is a carnival for the kids with rides, coin tosses, dart throws, cotton candy, clowns and more, lots of musical entertainment, the Clucky Chicken barn performance and the Fiddle Faddle Farm for the kids.

One event happens in the art pavilion. We have a People's Choice award which requires voting on the part of the visitors. This is a great way to meet people visiting the fair as you hand out the ballots. They vote for their favorite pieces and the two top winners receive $100 and $50 respectively.

Kids are wonderful. They love to vote and they have very strong opinions on which of the entries are their favorites. In the end we had 1600 votes to count. That took several hours to complete on Saturday evening, after closing time at nine.

Sunday was a little quiet. I guess there had been too much partying and fun earlier so it was slow on Sunday. Saturday had had the most attendees. We didn't have voting on the People's Choice on Sunday as we wanted to have the awards up on the paintings for the Sunday folks. Interaction with the visitors to the WPA barn to visit the art exhibit was more difficult, but we greeted them with a smile and asked if they had any questions, where they were from and how they happened to come to the fair. It was a chance to relax after more than a week of frenetic activity. Whew!

Monday folks came to pick up the piece of art that hadn't sold and, all in all, we considered it a successful show. We were picking up the remaining odds and ends, cleaning the space, taking down picture hangers and staples and generally tidying up this old building.

All the accouterments have been passed on to me and next year (if the virus permits) we will be off and running again with me as the full-fledged superintendent of the Fine Art category. Now all I have to do is get the information on the computer for next year, write the instructions for the premium books and be ready for July 2022!

Our Garden's Harvest for One Week

CHAPTER 21

The Fruits of Summer

"There is no fruit which is not bitter before it is ripe." — PubliliusSyrus

(This is a rant, so if you don't like rants, you can just skip this chapter. I try not to write rants too often, but occasionally one will pop up)

So here we are in the throes of summer. Earlier, in June, it was hot, very hot. Lots of plants had trouble coping with the heat as well as many of the people here in western Washington who think 80 degrees is too hot! In many cases it has stunted, sunburned or killed crops.

When I was a kid growing up in Redmond, Washington, it was rural countryside. Large vegetable gardens and orchards, Asian truck gardens, and folks who raised produce for the grocery and Pike Place Market were the norm and folks of this small rural community (700 people) were mostly small dairy farmers producing fruits and vegetables for their own use. Our five acre farm had a number of apple trees, most of which grew wild from seedlings. We used the apples for applesauce and made spiced applesauce cake as a regular staple for dessert. These small apples were also used with wild blackberries to make cobblers. They tasted fine and our horses thought that they were great treats, even though they didn't have a lot of eye appeal and were small.

On the old Bel-Redmond Road there was a ten acre peach orchard. When the peaches were ready, we would take our truck over to purchase several lugs (a box of 28 pounds of peaches) from the farmer who owned the trees. The redolent fragrance of peaches could be detected for several blocks before getting to the orchard. Unfortunately, that only lasted a few years when an early frost killed all the trees by bursting the trunks which were still full of sap. This was particularly sad as these were the sweetest, freestone peaches I have ever eaten.

We had cherry trees as well as a plum tree, though I didn't care for the latter as the skin was VERY sour. They were also probably self-sown seedlings as well. Of course, we had raspberries and strawberries and wild blackberries; which we made cobblers and jams and syrups and pies. What glories the summer fruits could bring.

This morning we had peaches for breakfast. Though I sorted through the fare at the grocery to find something ripe, it was still a disappointment, no flavor and cling-stoned fruit. Freestone peaches are hard to come by these days.

My rant is this:

In fact, most fruit has lost its delicious flavor in order to make the fruit longer lived and more shippable. Remember the red delicious apple from the 50s and 60s? It was delicious. Now it is a tough, bitter remnant of its former self, looking gorgeous in the display but with a skin that is more like leather and terribly bitter. I refuse to purchase them.

I have an acquaintance who is developing apples for market. He tells me that firstly, the apple must be shippable. What happened to flavor coming first? Isn't the most important thing about food THE FLAVOR? Or what about nutrition? What good is it if it tastes inferior, like this morning's peach? Are we growing this stuff to produce what I consider, in my opinion, to be chicken feed or garbage?

Avocados are hard as rocks and only about half of them ripen to the point of being edible. Mangos, ditto. The other half just turns black and tastes terrible. If you eat it too green, it doesn't have flavor.

Melons are too green to develop any flavor by ripening on the counter in your kitchen. Strawberries are often pithy and hollow, and lack flavor or sweetness even though they are gigantic and gorgeously red, but dead in flavor. Pineapples will ripen after purchase, so they are a somewhat safe bet. Mangos often turn black inside instead of ripening. Green tomatoes that have been "fumed" to make them turn red, they are still green tomatoes lacking flavor and aroma.

Why don't we grow food for taste instead of shipability? It is no wonder people don't eat their five fruits and veggies a day, they don't taste very good.

S
till Seeking a Place in the Country—Painting by D. Matzen

Epilogue

"My dream is to become a farmer. Just a Bohemian guy (gal) pulling up his own sweet potatoes for dinner." – Lenny Kravitz

We are still here on Whidbey, about fifty years after I first arrived looking for a place to be a pioneer. Bob and I still have our acreage and are living the good life. Luckily we are still well enough to be able to chop wood, beat back the pesky wild blackberries and enjoy our retirement.

You may have noticed that some of the vignettes mention my working, or still having chickens. Writing a memoir takes time and situations change. Yes, we have retired, which is good, because it takes us longer to accomplish all the things we could do easily when we were younger.

I am still painting and some of the examples are here in this book. I have more time to paint and experiment with other creative endeavors now that I am not teaching. COVID brought changes to our lives. My classes closed due to the virus. Zoom was too difficult for a hard-of-hearing person like me. I found that I really like retirement! So does my husband.

Now we can go camping whenever we like and we try to go some place about once a month except when it is to cold. We can go for longer trips now that I don't have twice a week classes. My former students are always trying to talk me into returning, but this is too much fun now and I like it.

When we wonder around Washington State, we dream of a new place to settle, but each has its advantages and disadvantages. Usually the disadvantages outweigh the advantages, so we enjoy visiting and dreaming that someday a perfect place will appear. In the meantime we enjoy the camping and visiting lots of places. Since we have visited many more than once, having liked them for a possible new farm, we also see that they are changing and have changed over the thirty years we have visited. Several of the places we tried to purchase years ago, we have revisited. Boy were we lucky those deals feel through. I guess we were pretty naïve back then thinking we could turn a rock pile into a farm.

Being closer to a large city has its advantages as you age as there are services available there that would be difficult to reach if we lived in the hinterland. We can be thankful that we still have the land that we bought so long ago, that we have the health and strength to tend to it, albeit to a lesser degree than in ages past. We can still see the stars occasionally though light pollution has dimmed the smaller ones. We can still sleep outside without the neighbors observing our weird habit. Though we have fewer animals, smaller gardens, and more trees, we are happy on our little farm on Whidbey.

Perhaps we should give up the search and make our lives here as comfortable and satisfying as possible. Forty plus years of accumulated goods would be a big project to move. It would require jettisoning a lot of superfluous stuff. Better stay in place.

Yes, rural America is vanishing, we see it every day, but change is inevitable. Keeps you on your toes!

Cowboy poetry may not be a favorite. Several years ago we were camping in Curlew, Washington and noticed that a local small brewery was having readings one evening. After reading the local newspaper and learning of wolves attacking cattle and farm foreclosures in the local region, I decided to write a piece for the reading. It is my first and only. I always like the poetry of Robert Service because it rhymes and has meter. Cowboy poetry also has rhyme and meter. We have been to several cowboy poetry readings in various rural locations, so here is the piece I wrote.

The Rancher's Wife

Work from dawn to setting sun,
The rancher's work is never done.
Milk the cow, geld the bull,
Ranching life is never dull

Pick the beans, gather eggs,
Clean the barn, repair the rigs.
Mow the field, bale the hay,
What to do rest of day?

To the bank to make a deal.
We need to buy another wheel.
Try to keep the wolves at bay.
And live to fight another day.

Little sleep at night from worry.
Get up early and start to hurry.
Line crews up and needs their grub,
Scrub laundry in a big tub.

Now its time to mend the fence.
How can those beeves be so dense
As to lean and pull and ravage them?
We could just lock them in the pen.

Calves get skinny and horses founder.
What business plan could be much sounder?
Sheep need dippin' and chicks are pippin',
The ranch wife's life ain't coffee sippin.

Traded satin for Sorrel boots
Long and far from my roots.
College never taught me this
But hard work brings me bliss.

In the heat of sun or the chill of snow
We are out at sunrise, on the go.
Rain and sleet, sweat and chill,
To give up ranching, 'never will.

You will have seen that some of these vignettes were produced a while back and some very recently. I am a full time painter and I do have a website where you may order my books, calendar, and peruse and purchase my paintings.

dcm@theruralgallery.com

www.theruralgallery.com

We still live on Whidbey and we are still seeking the perfect location to spend our old age if we have the energy to move.

Made in the USA
Columbia, SC
23 June 2023

18452957R40095